The Hours That Changed My Life

A CENTURION'S PERSPECTIVE

Mark S. Wilson

TRILOGY CHRISTIAN PUBLISHERS
TUSTIN, CA

Trilogy Christian Publishers
A Wholly Owned Subsidiary of Trinity Broadcasting Network
2442 Michelle Drive
Tustin, CA 92780

The Hours That Changed My Life

For information, address Trilogy Christian Publishing

Rights Department, 2442 Michelle Drive, Tustin, Ca 92780.

Trilogy Christian Publishing/ TBN and colophon are trademarks of Trinity Broadcasting Network.

For information about special discounts for bulk purchases, please contact Trilogy Christian Publishing.

Manufactured in the United States of America

10 9 8 7 6 5 4 3 2 1

Library of Congress Cataloging-in-Publication Data is available.

ISBN: 978-1-63769-994-2

E-ISBN: 978-1-63769-995-9

Contents

Dedication

My Father in heaven has graced me with two fathers here on earth, so to speak. Both of whom were like Centurions in my life. My dad, Jim Wilson, was the first "Centurion" during my formative years as a boy and eventually becoming a man. He watched over me and was the first to declare to me that Jesus is the Son of God. My father in the faith, Dr. Paul Risser, was also like a "Centurion" to me in my formative years in the ministry and as a man of God. He, too, watched over me and declared Jesus as the Son of God. I will be forever grateful to both of these men and the impact they had on my life.

Acknowledgments

Thank you...

To my wife, Joani, one of the Centurions in my life, who has been tested in the trenches of marriage and ministry with me for over thirty-nine years. Thanks for your help, support, and friendship all these years.

To my mother, Lavonne Wilson, who taught me to love God's Word and to read other books as well. You have been a huge inspiration in my life.

To my sisters, Valorie and Marci, for all your constant support and friendship. Again, let me apologize for being Mom and Dad's favorite.

To my eldest son, Brooks, who is as close to a real-life Centurion that I know and who crossed my mind several times while writing about Octavian.

To my son, Chad, who, along with his wife Jillian, are genuine Centurions, declaring Jesus at Hope Church in the community of Scotts Valley, CA.

To my Administrative Assistant, Lori Balog, for all your help with tenses and punctuation. I know my writing style drives you crazy, but you help make it better.

To David Ortega, my Associate Pastor, who has such a great knowledge of God's Word and Theology.

To Kolin Neilson and Janet Prince for all your help editing this book.

To Mike and Marty Greenwood, for your support and friendship over the years and for putting together a Tuesday lunch with Pastor Michael-John, which became a divine encounter, opening the doors for this book to be accepted and published by Trilogy Publishing.

To the Foothills Church in Gilroy, CA., some of my favorite people in the world and one of my favorite places to be. A place where I have formed the bonds of family as strong as blood relatives. You know who you are. Thank you for all of your support over our thirty-one years of ministry in the South Bay.

Preface

One morning, several months ago, I woke up and the first thought I had was to wonder what ever happened to the Centurion who was at the foot of the cross when Jesus died. The one who had proclaimed, "Surely this man was the Son of God!"[1] Immediately, I heard a voice inside me say, "Why don't you tell his story?" The voice, I believe, was the Lord, who usually speaks to me when I ask Him questions. So, I began that morning, a journey I had never really envisioned—writing a novel.

Sometimes we make things far more complicated than they need to be, especially when it pertains to the Christian experience. Being a follower of Christ is fairly simple when you think about it. We do what He tells us to do and then let Him bring about the results. I have attempted to do this with "The Hours That Changed My Life".

So the journey to write about this Centurion began. As time went on, I started to get an understanding of

---
[1] Mark 15:39 (NIV).

the type of man who would make such a powerful dec-laration. Even though my Centurion in this story is fictional, and I know it sounds weird, but I have come to consider him a friend. Like me, he was not perfect, and like me, he struggled with his issues of doubts and fears—and yet, growing in his love and admiration of Jesus Christ.

Writing about Octavian has made me more and more appreciative of the countless "Centurions" in my own life. People, who have in their own unique way, de-clared Jesus, the Son of God, to me. Without these peo-ple and their impact, I would never know Jesus the way I do today.

This novel has also made me aware of the fact that one of my primary roles on earth as a believer in Jesus is to declare Him as the Son of God to the people in my areas of influence.

As you read about Octavian, my hope is that a sense of appreciation, not only for Jesus but for the countless "Centurions" in your life, will grow. I also hope that you, too, will become more aware of the wonderful impact you can have on the people in your life.

I pray you enjoy meeting the two main characters in this story; Justus of the Decapolis, an avid searcher of truth, and Octavian, a man willing to share his story. An even deeper prayer of mine is that you fall more and more in love with Jesus, the hero of this novel. He not only died on a cross for you but rose to life and is return-ing soon to take His followers to our home in heaven.

CHAPTER 1

Justus

My name is Justus of the Decapolis, and I have been a follower of Jesus for some time now, even before His resurrection. I was born in the Decapolis, more specifically the town of Gerasa, which is just a little southeast of the Sea of Galilee. Gerasa, as with the other nine cities which form the Decapolis, is mainly populated by a mixture of Greeks and Jews. Thus, being a perfect description of my family, both Greek and Jewish. My father was Greek, and he passed away several years ago. My mother is still alive, and being of Jewish origin, a follower of Jehovah. My father used to scoff at my mother for following what he called "her invisible God". He said there were no other gods but the Emperor. In spite of my father's disposition toward my mother's God, she was as faithful to Jehovah as she could be and continues even more so in her devotion to the Lord. She would try to teach me things from the Scriptures, but I was never very interested. My father's influence over my thinking and beliefs, as I assume most are, was much stronger than my mother's influence.

When my father became ill, my mother and I would pray to Jehovah, asking for my father to be healed. She would tell me of the love and power of her God, but her God either did not listen or was powerless to help. In my young mind, because my father died, it became clear to me that Jehovah did not love me and that He was powerless to help me. After my father's funeral, out of my anger and disappointment, I completely rejected my mother's God, left my home, and went in search of happiness and pleasure.

As time went by, I found myself further and further away from my mother's beliefs as I followed the hedonistic teachings and ways of the Greeks. Sinking deeper into sin, I began to dabble in all sorts of evil. The deeper I sank, the more this evil took hold of me. I turned into a violent and terribly mean man. Eventually, I became so depressed; I had thoughts of ending my life. My mental state was so bad, and I became such a horrible person, it was impossible for anyone to be around me. I was in and out of jail for assault, burglary, and disturbing the peace. Toward the end of what was quickly becoming a way of life for me, I was driven away from society because of my mental instability and violent tendencies and ended up living in the tombs of the Gerasenes. Later, after Jesus healed me, I learned I was possessed by many demons. Jesus called them a "legion". Looking back on it now, I am so glad my mother didn't see me in that condition. It would have, or should I say, "I," would have broken her heart.

My encounter with Jesus happened one day while I was raving mad and roaming in those tombs. I was not fully aware of many things at that time because of my demonic condition, but that day, when I saw a boat approaching the shore of the Sea of Galilee, my hostility and curiosity were peaked. I saw a man getting off the boat. He was followed by some other men, but I scarcely noticed them. All my focus was on the first man who was in the lead. I do not know how, but somehow, I felt drawn to this man who was approaching. I knew this man was my only hope. I rushed to Him, probably shouting what was some nonsense, and fell at His feet. Jesus simply commanded the many demons who had been a part of me to come out of me. At that very instant, with just His word, Jesus set me free from my bondage to sin, delivered me from the demons who had tortured me for years, and completely restored my sanity. I had never been so happy, free, and at peace in my life. My mother was right all along, the Messiah was coming to rescue us, and I had just met Him!

Right after my deliverance, as I was sitting and in my right mind, for the first time in years, I begged Jesus to allow me to follow Him wherever He went. Jesus had a better idea—He told me to return to my home region of the Decapolis and tell everyone all the good things He had done for me. As Jesus and I, along with His disciples, walked toward the shoreline, I couldn't take my eyes off Him. My heart had never been so full of gratitude and wonder! As the disciples were climbing into the boat, Jesus stopped and put both hands on my shoulders. He looked me directly in the eyes and told me He loved me and that the Spirit of Jehovah would be with me and not to fear. Then He said something that just melted my heart in my chest. He told me Jehovah did, in fact, love me very much and that He had great power to help me. He then urged me to start praying again to Jehovah and that He is always listening. I didn't know what to say. My eyes teared up as I remembered what I thought about my mother's God after my father died. Jesus gently shook me and seemingly looked deep within my soul and again said those impactful words. My heart felt so cleansed by His words. I then asked Jesus why they had come to the tombs that day, and He simply said, "For you, Justus."

I watched as the boat grew smaller and smaller on the horizon. I packed up what little possessions I had and began my journey back home to my mother.

When I finally reached home, my mother, with tears streaming down her face, met me at the door and we embraced. It was so good to be home again finally, but this time without anger. I felt only peace. My mother could sense this peace and asked me what had happened. This was my first opportunity to share what Jesus had done for me. Wanting to spare her feelings, I didn't go into all the details of who I had become since I had left home. I mainly focused on what Jesus did for me and who He was to me now—the Messiah she had long been awaiting. Obviously, my mother was relieved and overjoyed by all I told her. She has now put her faith, not only in Jehovah but in His Son Jesus, our Messiah.

I have found this to be the best strategy when I tell people my story. To keep the focus on Jesus and not myself. Since my awakening and salvation, I have been doing this very thing, telling people about Jesus. It is my mission. As a result, there are a number of people who follow Jesus in my hometown and the other nine cities of the Decapolis. I have been appointed the leader of the fellowships that meet in various homes throughout the week. Some of the followers call me "teacher," which really embarrasses me.

Me, a teacher? If they only knew the person I was before I met Jesus and all the evil that I had done in my past, they might not think of me as a teacher of anything good—but this is the power of Jesus in our lives. The person I once was, is no longer relevant. What is important now is who I am becoming through Him and because of Him. All I want to do is serve Him and care for others because of what Jesus did in healing and restoring me. One aspect of my service to Jesus is to be a witness of all He has done for me, just as He instructed. The other aspect of my service is to learn as much as possible from other followers about their encounters with Jesus, so I can teach their stories at our gatherings in the Decapolis.

It is for this reason that I have traveled to Jerusalem. I had frequented the city of David a number of times since the death, burial, and resurrection of Jesus because I wanted to stay connected with the gatherings of the twelve disciples. I have developed a relationship with these twelve men and many others. A number of the Twelve (as I often refer to them) recognized me from my encounter with Jesus at the tombs when I first walked into one of their meetings. The Twelve and many, many others gather regularly in the various homes of the followers to teach about Jesus, pray, and encourage one another.

Typically, one or more of the twelve will share something Jesus said or tell a story about Jesus. Others are welcome to share, but there are some rules that are strictly enforced. If a person shares their story, it must be about Jesus, and there needs to be an eyewitness. If a person relays something Jesus said, they have to have heard it themselves, and it must be confirmed by at least one other follower. The Twelve are very protective of the reputation of Christ and their burgeoning church. They also know too well the slimy tactics of the Pharisees, who are always trying to twist Jesus' words. The Pharisees also try hard to discredit all the disciples of Jesus in order to stop their gatherings. The Twelve are very careful not to let any of the old religious ways, which Jesus rejected, to infiltrate the Church.

It was a pleasantly warm summer evening when I made my way to this particular gathering. Upon arriving at the place, the home was quaint, nothing fancy, just a good, solid home, similar to the many homes lining the streets of Jerusalem. It was very inviting, and I felt a peaceful presence as I walked through the gate and into the courtyard. The meeting area was inside the house with large windows that opened up to the beautiful courtyard facing the street. The courtyard maximized the space, so one could see and hear both inside and outside the dwelling. I saw John almost immediately, standing in the courtyard talking to another follower. John and I had become fast friends since the first time I went to a meeting after the resurrection of Jesus. It is difficult not to be friends with John; he is a very loving man to everyone. He and Andrew are like the welcoming committee for all the gatherings. I have never met men as kind as John and Andrew. The other disciples are great too, but I have a special bond with John and Andrew. You can tell the disciples have spent considerable time with Jesus because they act a lot like Him. John tells me this is our real mission of life—to be like Jesus and love people.

After John and I exchanged greetings, I told him that I had come to meet the man, the very man—the Centurion who was at the foot of the cross when Jesus died. John said he knew him and that they were good friends. Why was I not surprised? He looked around the meeting place and said he had not seen him as of yet but that it was still early. I asked if he would let me know when he arrived. John said, "When he arrives, he will be difficult to miss." He saw the quizzical look on my face and simply said, with a slight smile forming on his lips, "Trust me, you will know."

As I made my way around the gathering, I saw other friends and greeted them, but inwardly I prayed, "O Lord, please send him here tonight."

It had been several months since Jesus was crucified and rose from the dead. There was still a considerable buzz concerning the events of that day and the days following. The gatherings of the Twelve were growing larger and larger by the day, and many people of all walks of life were finding Jesus as their Savior.

I saw Mary of Clopas, and she said John had told her I was looking for the Centurion and that the two were friends. She said the few who were at the cross when Jesus died had a strong connection with one another and that if the Centurion, whom she said was named Octavian, showed up, she would point him out to me. Mary Magdalene also came up to me and said she was on the lookout for him as well. I knew for certain now that if the Centurion was at the gathering that night, I would meet him. I was so excited at the possibility and prayed again, "Lord, please send him here tonight."

Shortly after the meeting had begun, Mary of Clopas gently nudged me and pointed him out to me as he walked in. Of course! That had to be him. John was right. There was just something about him that was different. He wasn't wearing his uniform, but you could tell he was a soldier, and not just an ordinary soldier, a commander of men. It was the way he carried himself. His stride and stature spoke of absolute confidence and fearlessness. There was definitely an aura about him, but not one of arrogance. Octavian had authority to his presence. He had this look of a man with whom you would not want to trifle with.

I had to gather myself when I saw him because I so wanted to meet him at that moment, but I would have to wait until the meeting was over. I was so anxious to speak with him—the very man who was the last person to see our Jesus alive and to hear our Lord's final words. I had come a long way to learn everything I could from him and confirm some of the things being reported. There were a lot of rumors and falsehoods being spread about Jesus' arrest, crucifixion, and what He said on the cross. This was why I sought out this Centurion. He was an actual eyewitness of the last few hours of Jesus' life—the last hours that changed the world, but for now, I would have to wait.

As the meeting went on, I stole several glances at him. He was listening so intently, which I found impressive. Everything about him was impressive. To see a Roman at a meeting of a bunch of Jews was extraordinary. I fought the urge to just run over to him and introduce myself, but then again, I thought it probably wouldn't be wise to run up to any Centurion, a believer in Jesus or not.

After the final prayer of the evening, I, along with the two Marys, approached him. I followed behind them because I was a little intimidated. After all, he was a Centurion. The two Marys, on the other hand, were not the least bit afraid. They just walked toward him and loudly exclaimed, "Brother Octavian!" The three of them embraced as I stood back, a little nervous. They turned and introduced me to Octavian and then told him why I had come to the meeting. He nodded politely and stretched out his rather large and muscular hand. I extended mine, and when he shook my hand, I had never felt so small and weak. He had a powerful grip.

After our, well his, hearty hand shake, Octavian said, "Hello, it's a pleasure to meet you." I could not have been more surprised. His kind and gentle voice belied his stern and gruff demeanor. The other remarkable feature of this Centurion was his eyes. His eyes were full of life and depth. His eyes revealed a light and excitement that only those who had discovered gold or had an encounter with Jesus Christ would know. I was a little dumbfounded, standing before this imposing Centurion, but I finally managed to say, "Hello, the pleasure is all mine."

Centurions, as most people in Israel know, are highly respected soldiers. They are literally the tip of Rome's spear. There is a saying in Rome that it is rare to find an old Centurion because they are warriors first and officers second. Centurions are the commanders who actually lead their soldiers into battle, and so the mortality rate for them was extremely high. Although a little weather-beaten and worn, Octavian was still an impressive man. I could not tell how old he was, but as Centurions go, he was the oldest I had ever come across.

I also dared not ask him about his service in the Roman Legion, even though I was fascinated by history, for I thought that might be a sensitive subject for someone who had obviously seen war. As for his appearance, Octavian was of average height, but there was nothing average about his build. He was solid from head to toe, like a rock cut from the quarry. He had olive skin that was well tanned, like a man who made his living in the fields. His eyes were hazel brown and full of life and depth, and just from looking into them, you could tell he was a serious man. He had salt and pepper hair, which was cut short, and as most Romans of his day, he had no facial hair, only a slight bit of stubble that dotted his square jaw line. Octavian also had a pronounced scar that ran just under the left eye and across his crooked nose, obviously from some sort of scuffle. The lines on his face were like a road map of Rome's military campaigns, and I'm sure he witnessed many in his days as a soldier.

Centurions did not rise to their rank without battle experience, heroism, and courage. His first knowledge and experience in war, although I'm sure it was fascinating, was not my concern this evening. What I wanted to ask him about was his firsthand knowledge of the death, burial, and resurrection of Jesus Christ.

With the introduction out of the way, I briefly told him about my personal experience with Jesus in the tombs of the Gerasenes. I also told him about our gatherings in the Decapolis and my reason for coming to Jerusalem. He seemed very interested as I spoke of my encounter with Jesus, almost as if he was trying to learn all he could about our Messiah, which was my life's mission. What I have discovered about many seekers of Jesus is that they want to learn all they can about Him. I further explained to Octavian that as one of the leaders in the Decapolis gatherings, I was trying to talk with as many people as I could who were eyewitnesses of what Jesus said and did. I told him that his encounter with Jesus was of great interest to me and the group of followers back home. Even though it was fairly late in the evening, I asked him if he had a few moments to speak with me about his experience with Jesus. He readily agreed, as if excited to speak of the Messiah given any chance or reason. We ended up speaking together for some time, and I furiously wrote every word of his encounter. The following is what I have gathered from our meeting and his eyewitness account.

CHAPTER 2

The Centurion

The two Marys could see we were getting along well enough, and so they excused themselves and went off to talk with the many other followers of Christ who had attended the meeting. I spotted a table and chairs near the corner of the meeting place and motioned we go over. We began making our way, and as we did, I noticed the disciple John smile and wave. I could see he was excited that Octavian and I had been introduced. I started to sit down, but the Centurion politely, yet firmly said, "I prefer to sit there. I will only sit with my back against the wall unless I am accompanied by a fellow Centurion." I apologized and moved to the other chair, and as we sat down, me in the "right" seat, I asked as I was pulling out my writing kit if I could write down what he was going to tell me? He nodded and said emphatically, "It should be done. There should be a record of everything I have seen and heard surrounding the crucifixion of Jesus." He went on to say he had thought about telling his story and that he had shared a few things with John and Andrew, but nothing formal had been set up.

He seemed relieved to be able to talk with someone about his experience. He even said he was grateful that I had come to meet with him and then shrugged and said, "In my line of work, one never knows how much time they have left." I sort of chuckled and said, "None of us knows, right?"

I told Octavian that I was a little nervous and not to take offense, but I was dying to know something about Centurions and if he would indulge me in a silly question before we start. Inwardly, I thought he was a little nervous too, so I was trying to ease the tensions at the table. With pursed lips and a puzzled look, Octavian nodded his head and said, "Sure, ask away." I thanked him and said, "It's about the helmet you wear. I understand the need for a helmet, but why do you have the plume on the top, and why does the Centurion's plume go side to side on the helmet and not front to back like the other soldiers?" He laughed. I could see my plan of easing things was already working. "As to the last part of your question, our horse hairs or brushes go side to side because we are not any other soldier; we are Centurions. The other reason we have them is so we can be easily identified by our men on the battlefield. Centurions are out in front of the soldiers and not in the rear, so when they see our brushes, they follow. The soldiers under me must be able to find me at all times. Also, if a brother Centurion goes down on the battlefield, his troops are instructed to find another Centurion to rally behind. Our brushes serve as a rallying point during the fight because where a Centurion is, so is the fight. The downside to our horse hairs is that the approaching enemy can also quickly identify the Centurions. That is why we are the best and most feared warriors in the Roman Legion. The horse hairs also help us locate our fellow Centurions on the battlefield in order to lend assistance if we see they are in trouble or signal them if we are in trouble ourselves. When we are not on the battlefield and stationed in an occupied area like Jerusalem, our brushes serve to intimidate the crowds when we are on duty."

I thanked him again for answering my silly question, to which he smiled and raised a hand as if to say no problem. I told him I had always wanted to know what they meant, and that I had thought about just asking a Centurion but could never muster the courage. He said, "It is probably a good thing you never mustered up the courage." With that, he chuckled, and I said, "You are probably right." Good, I thought, job done. The tension had lifted, and we were ready to proceed, so I asked him if he would mind starting off by telling me a little about himself.

In a somewhat formal way, the Centurion cleared his throat and began by telling me that his name was

Octavian Calidus. He said he was named Octavian by his parents after the first Roman Emperor. Calidus had come from the fact that he used to be quite hot headed and reckless. That, he said, had gotten better since he met Jesus. He went on to say, "My parents thought naming me Octavian might mean I would be a ruler someday. But the Calidus in me deemed me to be fit only as a soldier. As it is, I am a Centurion and one of sixty Cohorts in Rome's fourth Legion. I have 100 men under my charge, and I was stationed in Jerusalem during the time of the crucifixion of Jesus of Nazareth."

"For the record," I asked, "You were the Centurion with Jesus at the end?" "That is correct," he replied, and with that, Octavian spoke extensively about all he experienced. He went on to say...

"I was the Centurion at the foot of the cross when Jesus breathed His last. I say 'breathed His last' because I do not think He died in the natural way of suffocation from the hours on a cross. I also know for a fact that He did not die from His legs being broken or from the spear in His side. The spear that pierced His side only confirmed that He had expired. I know because I saw the blood, mixed with water, flow out from the wound."

"So, Jesus breathed His last by choice?" I asked. "Yes, it was His choosing to die and not by anything we did to Him. It was a death unlike any I have ever witnessed.

At the point of His death, He just said, 'It is finished,'[2] bowed His head, and it was over. I have never come across another person in the world who had such control over themselves and seemed so unaffected by the events and actions surrounding Him. Even in death, He had such command and presence. I have had it confirmed from some of His disciples, John to be specific, that Jesus basically said, no one could take His life from Him and that He alone had the authority over His life.[3] From where I stood, this is the truth of what happened when Jesus said those final three words."

Octavian continued, "When Jesus said those words, 'It is finished,' there was such a look of satisfaction in His eyes—Like a painter who had just put the finishing touches on a masterpiece."

Visibly, Octavian was moved with emotion as he sat back in his chair. He seemed to drift off in thought, and then he said, "I could have sworn He looked right at me. I will never forget that. Those indeed were the hours that changed my life. That day and the events leading up to it will be ingrained in my memory for the rest of my life. That is the thing about truth... about Jesus, as I have come to learn. The truth, nor a genuine encounter with Him, will ever leave you. He cannot be forgotten, especially if you made eye contact with Him. His

---

[2] John 19:30 (NIV).
[3] John 10:17-18.

eyes were unforgettable. Many of us have spoken with each other about this since the resurrection. It's almost as though you can spot one of His followers because of their eyes. Anyone who has come to know Jesus as their Savior has the same light shining in their eyes."

Octavian then said, "When we were introduced, I knew you too had an encounter with Jesus." As he was saying this to me, I thought back to my brief time with Jesus and the way He looked at me—Like He knew everything I had ever said or done. All the sin and evil and hurt I had committed to myself and others, and yet there was no judgment, only love looking back at me. I told Octavian that I couldn't agree more. There was something about Jesus' eyes that could not be forgotten.

Octavian continued, "The truth is, I saw Jesus die and saw the blood mixed with water flow from His side.[4] I know there are those who say Jesus never did, in fact, die because they cannot explain His resurrection, but I testify with certainty, He died on that cross. I was there and would challenge or fight anyone who says differently. I still have some of my Calidus tendencies. The other remarkable thing about Jesus on the cross and during the proceedings of the trials was that He never whined, cursed, complained, or made threats like all the other criminals I have witnessed during a crucifixion. You really find out just how tough, or should I say "fake" tough,

---

[4] John 19:34-35.

criminals are when faced with death. Not Jesus! I have never seen a man in such agony die with such grace. The disciple John tells us Jesus is full of grace."[5]

I then asked Octavian if he had heard about Jesus before the day of the arrest or if that was the first he had heard or seen of Him. He answered, "Oh yes, Jesus was well known! Many of my fellow soldiers had encountered Him. His name would come up in the barracks, especially around Passover week when He would come into the city. There was always chaos when He came—but not that Jesus was the cause of it, only that there were multitudes following Him and trying to get close to Him. I realize now why the people wanted to be near Him, but at the time, I could not understand why so many wanted to know some religious teacher."

At this, Octavian paused and with a sigh said, "Oh, how we hated those Jews and all their religious festivals and ceremonies, their sacrifices and rituals. A pure waste of time, in my opinion, for all the good it did for them. They always seemed so phony and ridiculous to me. I'm not so sure their religion meant that much to them either. Many Jews use their festivals as either an excuse to make money or to cause trouble. The other thing about their festivals and ceremonies is, they never seemed to bring the Jews much joy to their lives. They were so intent on following every rule and making the

---

[5] John 1:14.

Pharisees happy that it ruined their celebrations. You'd think their religion would mean more to them and do more for them, but it didn't seem that way to me. What I really hated about their festivals and celebrations, in Jerusalem especially, was all the extra work they caused for my soldiers and me. There was always a lot more tension in the city because of the crowds that gathered. The Passover week, just before Jesus' arrest and crucifixion, was extremely difficult. There was so much excitement in the air over Him. Jews from everywhere were flooding the marketplaces and the temple area just to catch a glimpse or even touch 'The Healer'. This was the name that He was given by some of the soldiers—'The Healer'. At first, it was meant as a joke. Uh... until you met Jesus and actually saw Him heal people. That was no joke! One of my fellow Centurions, Lucius, who used to mock Jesus a lot, was on duty watching over a crowd where Jesus was speaking. He said Jesus healed a blind man and then looked right at him, smiled and winked, but not in a judgmental way. Lucius said it was the kindest reprimand he ever received, and that he was sick to his stomach for a couple of days. After that, Lucius never mocked Jesus again."

While Octavian was talking about Lucius' encounter with Jesus, I was reminded of another rumor I had heard a while back, and so I asked him about it. I told Octavian that I had heard Jesus healed the servant of a

Centurion in Capernaum and asked him if he knew the man or had heard of the story.

"Absolutely, I have heard the story of Jesus healing the Centurion's servant. I do not know the man, but it was said that he impressed Jesus by the way he responded to Him." He went on to say, "I heard the Centurion said, 'Just say the word, and it will happen'[6] or something to that effect. I completely understand why that Centurion responded to Jesus in the way he did. It is how we Centurions have to live our lives and how we survive in battle. Our words and actions must be in one accord. If a Centurion says something, then it must be done. Our credibility with our soldiers helps to keep us alive and keeps them following us in battle. As I progress in my faith in Jesus, I am learning that this, too, is what real faith requires. Our words must line up with our actions, or our credibility is gone. The only thing I found odd at the time of hearing about this Centurion's encounter with Jesus was not what he said but how any Roman Centurion would refer to Jesus as a fellow officer or his commander. Certainly, I understand it now."

As Octavian was speaking, I was struck by how impressive these Centurions were. I had always hated them in the past. They were frightening men and sometimes quite cruel to the Jews and even to their soldiers. However, listening to Octavian, you realize they are just

---

[6] Matthew 8:8.

men with problems of their own, doing a difficult job. I asked Octavian if he knew the name of the Centurion from Capernaum, but he said he did not. I thought to myself that I might have to take a trip over there soon and see if I could find him. I'd love to hear about his encounter with Jesus too.

I apologized to Octavian for getting him off track and asked him to continue talking about the days leading up to Jesus' arrest and the crowds He attracted in Jerusalem.

He said, "That's right, the crowds. Like I said, the Jewish festivals were a problem for us Romans. There was always so much activity surrounding them. For the most part, there was order, but the number of people who came from all over Israel caused a lot of friction. Then there were the threats of the Zealots who were hidden in plain sight by the masses the festivals attracted. A Roman soldier literally had to watch his back from those cutthroat weasels. Rumor had it that Jesus had a Zealot as one of His disciples. It was also said He had a tax collector with Him. I found it strange that He had such a diverse group of followers. Zealots, tax collectors, prostitutes, and fishermen… Everyone seemed welcomed by Him. I guess you could add Roman soldiers to that list of followers as well because I, too, have become one of Jesus' diverse group.

That particular Passover week, the one leading up to Jesus' arrest, was very chaotic. The crowds were bigger than ever because of the popularity of Jesus. I wasn't on duty the first day of the week, but I heard that Jesus entered the city, causing quite a stir. He rode in on a donkey, and the people shouted and proclaimed Him their King.[7] From what I was told by Rufus, the Centurion who was on duty that day, the Pharisees were all upset about the people praising Jesus and that they tried to get his soldiers to quiet the people down and keep them from shouting.[8] He was laughing when he told me. He also said he laughed at them." In an exasperated tone, Octavian continued, "Those Pharisees, they were such a thorn in our sides. It still amazes me that in just a few days, that crowd of Jews went from shouting 'Hosanna, Hosanna' to 'Crucify, Crucify'. But that was the power and influence the Pharisees held over the people. No offense, but the Jews are a fickle lot. They were so afraid of their religious leaders, the Pharisees, I mean, like they were 'gods'. We knew different, though. We had seen who they really were and knew they were as lost as those they condemned."

Octavian reflected for a moment and said, "My heart has softened a little toward the Pharisees because of Jesus. The longer you know Him, the more you realize you

---

[7] John 12:12-15.
[8] Luke 19:36-40.

have the same sinful tendencies as everyone else, and so you judge others less harshly. I still struggle with the Pharisees. I have heard from the disciples of Jesus that He struggled with them too. There is nothing worse than dealing with people who think they are good and everyone else is evil, especially when it is clearly visible that they were not as good as they thought. This is why we hated the Pharisees. They thought too highly of themselves and too lowly of everyone else."

I told Octavian I agreed with him on that point. I, too, had dealings with the Pharisees back in the Decapolis, and they were always trying to disrupt our gatherings and called us all sorts of derogatory names for following Jesus. I said it was a struggle for me to love them as well, but John reminds me, Jesus is love.

Octavian went on to tell me some other things he knew about Jesus before the crucifixion. "We heard a lot of things about Him. News of Him traveled fast. We heard of Him healing people, feeding multitudes, and raising people from the dead. There were even some of my fellow soldiers who secretly became His followers. I, on the other hand, was fairly indifferent to Jesus. I didn't have a problem with Him; I just didn't want Him causing any trouble or more work for my soldiers and myself. When He was in town, we were all on high alert. The other thing about Jesus was that I was a little suspicious of any Jew, especially one who made the Divine claims He had been making. I had more of a "let's wait and see" attitude toward Him. Mostly when the topic of Jesus came up, I inwardly hoped He wasn't coming to Jerusalem when I was on duty. And if He was, then I just wanted to get through all the madness while He was in town. There always seemed to be an uproar when Jesus came to Jerusalem. To be fair, Jesus never caused a single problem that I am aware of, but when thousands are trying to see and hear Him, it can become a frantic and dangerous situation."

Octavian then said, "You know I heard Jesus speak once? I was on duty near where He was talking to a large crowd. He was very impressive, but not in an intimidating way. Not that there were many Jews that could intimidate a Roman soldier or cause him to be afraid, but if there were, He was certainly one. There was just something about Him. There was a power and authority to Him that is difficult to describe. He wasn't exceptionally large in stature. In fact, there was nothing impressive in His appearance that drew you to Him.[9] He was very fit and strong, but that is not what defined His power. His gait was confident, and His eyes were penetrating—like He saw through everyone and everything. The few times I saw Him, He always seemed to be in complete control, He never seemed in a hurry, and never did He appear flustered or surprised. It was like

---

[9] Isaiah 53:2.

He knew what was happening at a deeper level than everyone else. Especially that night, the night of His arrest, and the hours that followed."

I found it very enlightening to learn so much about Jesus from a Roman's perspective. Octavian had a unique point of view that was proving to be helpful in my understanding. I commented to Octavian that it seemed Jesus had not only an effect on Israel but on all of Rome. Octavian nodded his head in agreement and said, "He was one of the most talked about figures of the day. I think that's one of the reasons why the Pharisees hated Jesus so much and why some of the officials in Rome were cautious of Him. All of that became quite clear on the night I was summoned to accompany a group of Pharisees and Jewish leaders to the Garden of Gethsemane to arrest Him."

I then told Octavian how appreciative I was to hear his perspective and that I hoped it wasn't too late in the evening because I was anxious to hear about the arrest. Octavian reassured me that it was his pleasure and that he was grateful to be able to share his account of what happened.

With that, Octavian proceeded...

CHAPTER 3

The Arrest

Pausing and clearing his throat, Octavian shifted his weight in his chair and his mood changed. He became very serious and almost looked angry. I sat back and swallowed hard. He definitely transformed, right before my eyes, from brother Octavian to a Centurion. It was clear to me then how Rome had conquered the world; it was because of soldiers like Octavian. In spite of the tension in the air, I nervously asked him if he was alright and if he wanted to continue. He lifted his head, looked at me, and I felt a little scolded by the look in his eyes. Then he said, "I don't talk too often about it, but I was there that night, and it still makes me angry." Even the tone of his voice changed, I thought.

Octavian continued, "I hate what 'we,' no, I can't speak for anyone else, what 'I' did to Jesus and all that happened in those hours. I realize, however, that had I not been there, I may never have met my Savior. I am still working through all of my emotions over the whole ordeal." I feigned a look of surprise as he kept going.

"I was on duty that evening and was at the Praetorium when I was commanded to report to Vitalis, the Primi Ordines at Jerusalem."

I interrupted Octavian and asked him what or who the Primi Ordines was, and he simply said, "He was the Centurion over ten Cohorts in the Roman Legion, his being the first, and that he was his commanding officer." I said thank you and apologized because I had never heard of the term. Octavian said, "No problem," and then continued.

"Vitalis' quarters were nearby. I hurried over to see what he needed. I was a little taken aback by the command because of the late hour and the urgency to which he had summoned me. When I arrived, Vitalis ordered me to go with a group of Pharisees and Jewish elders to the Garden of Gethsemane and arrest Jesus of Nazareth. I didn't show it, but this really bothered me. As a Centurion assigned to Jerusalem for some time now, my men and I had arrested many people, and at all hours of the day and night, but never at the behest of the Pharisees. I took my orders from Rome and not from those phony religious leaders, but mine was not to question a command, only to follow. So, I gathered a detachment of soldiers and met up with the group of Jewish leaders who were waiting outside the Praetorium. Immediately the Jews had an attitude with me because they thought I should have been in more of a hurry. Man, I tell you, had I not been under Vatalis' orders, those Jewish leaders would have been arrested that night and not Jesus. I do not like attitude from any subordinate."

I looked at Octavian's scowl and thought to myself, *Who did those Pharisees think they were to give attitude to this intimidating Centurion?*

Octavian continued, "The whole thing was a sham! Those Pharisees were all upset over Jesus, and none of us could really figure out why. As far as any of us knew, He had never done anything deserving arrest. All we ever saw or heard of Him was that He helped people. To us, He was no threat to Rome or Israel. Anyway, all the way to the Garden, the Pharisees kept going on and on about how Jesus had blasphemed their God and didn't follow their rules. My men and I looked at each other and smirked. We found that statement amusing coming from them. They seemed pretty blasphemous to us and not too keen on following the rules they wanted everyone else to follow, but that is the way it is with most people in power, Jewish or not. They told us they had paid one of His followers to point Jesus out to us, but even that was ludicrous. We knew who Jesus was—pretty much everyone knew who He was. Anyone who saw Him never forgot Him, and that's just it, He was unforgettable, however, those ridiculous Pharisees had their silly little protocols."

There was a slight breeze in the air that evening, and it was a chilly night. It also was very dark. Only our torches enabled us to see anything. It was oddly dark too. Like darkness I had never felt, and that was it, I felt the darkness. As we were approaching the Garden's entrance, the disciple named Judas was pushed toward the front of the group as though he were leading the detachment. Even though it was difficult to see, we could still make out the grove of olive trees and a solitary figure just standing there, like He expected us. He stepped forward, and I immediately knew it was Jesus. A number of other men, His disciples, I presumed, having been stirred from their sleep, appeared bewildered by what was happening. Judas walked toward Jesus, and Jesus said something to him that I was unable to hear, and then unpredictably, Judas kissed Jesus on the cheek. I was told later by the disciples that Judas had followed Jesus for a few years and had become frustrated with Jesus' non-violent ways and that Judas wanted Jesus to lead the charge against Rome and win back Israel's freedom. That was not what Jesus came to do. He came to set all people free, not from the tyranny of Rome, but from the tyranny of sin."

I told Octavian that Judas did an unthinkable act and that the disciples still couldn't believe he would do something so heinous. Octavian shook his head and then said, "After Judas kissed Jesus, Jesus looked past him and asked us, 'Who are you looking for'? One of the Pharisees said, 'Jesus of Nazareth.' Jesus took a step forward and said, 'I AM HE!'[10] When those words came out of His mouth, it was like a bolt of lightning went through me. Immediately I was face down on the ground. Everyone else in the Garden was down as well because as I slowly tried to lift my head off the dirt floor of the Garden, all I could see was Jesus. He was the only one standing. It was like all of our strength and energy were sucked out of us. As we were getting up, there was Jesus, waiting patiently and calmly, like He knew what was going on while the rest of us were in the dark, literally and figuratively. Myself, along with the soldiers with me, were wondering what happened and why Jesus didn't run away while we were on the ground. Obviously, we couldn't have caught Him; we could barely stand, but He just stood there. After we slowly rose to our feet again and still feeling a little wobbly, we started to approach Him. This was when one of His followers grabbed a sword, Peter, I was later informed, and cut this guy's ear off, right in front of us.[11] We were still a little shaken up, and so we didn't react quickly enough. Then something amazing happened! There was some screaming and shouting, and my men were starting to draw their swords as tensions grew high. Jesus, in com-

---

[10] John 18:4-5 (NIV).
[11] John 18:10.

THE HOURS THAT CHANGED MY LIFE

plete calm and composure, went over to the bleeding man and put his ear back in its place. Instantly he was healed![12] We stood frozen; mouths opened, shocked. I wondered... *What were we doing here, and who was this man we were sent to arrest?*

I blurted out, "What! Peter cut a guy's ear off!" Octavian nodded, and a smile crept over his face. He went on to say Peter still feels ashamed over the incident and that he likes to tease Peter every now and again about the ear. I laughed and said, "I've never heard Peter mention it." Octavian said, "And you probably won't." I asked Octavian if he ever saw the man whose ear was cut off. Octavian said, "I saw that guy the same night at the trial. Someone said he was a servant of one of the Pharisees. I always wondered what he thought afterward about his healing. I know I would never look at him or his ear the same way again."

"After Jesus healed the servant's ear, all of His disciples scattered and left Him all alone, but even that didn't shock Him. Nothing seemed to rattle Jesus. It was like everything was taking place at a slower pace for Him than it was for everyone else. It was like He knew what was happening and what was going to happen. Like a statue, Jesus stood in the middle of the Garden, no protesting or attempts to run, no whining or crying. Just silent, like a lamb before the shearer.[13] I have to be

---

[12] Luke 22:50-51.
[13] Isaiah 53:7.

honest with you; I borrowed that line from one of your Prophets—Isaiah, I think it was. Peter was talking about that passage a few days ago. As Peter read the prophet's words, it was exactly what had taken place at the arrest and later on at the trial. Even though I had never heard Isaiah's words before, they sounded so familiar to me—like I was there... which I was! Jesus silently took it all with such incredible composure. He was being very cooperative in the Garden. Oh, but make no mistake about it; there was something else about Jesus that put me on edge. I was watching Him very closely now, and He turned His gaze to me. Our eyes locked, and He had a look in His eyes, a look I had seen before."

"Years ago, when I was a mere soldier, I was on duty in whatever desert Rome had sent us to at that time. The sun was setting as I was starting my watch, when all of a sudden, a male lion emerged from a thicket only a few paces away from me. We squared off for a brief moment as I slowly drew my sword. Thankfully, the lion turned and ambled off, but I will never forget that evening and those eyes looking back at me. Jesus had those same eyes. He may have had the demeanor and heart of a lamb, but He had the eyes of a lion. Unnerved a little by Jesus' stare, I put my hand on the pommel of my sword and ordered my men to stay alert. I returned His gaze with my own, trying to be as intimidating as possible, but Jesus, just like that lion, seemed unfazed.

One of the Pharisees then said, 'Well, aren't you going to arrest Him?' Not knowing which Pharisee spoke, for my eyes did not leave this man standing before me, I barked at them all to shut their mouths and step back, to which they feigned outrage and offense, but I didn't care. Jesus may have fooled them into thinking He was weak like they were, but He wasn't. I decided right then to proceed with caution, for this was not some "religious leader". I then ordered one of my men to tie His hands. Jesus, whose eyes never left mine, calmly and with great poise extended His hands, almost inviting the straps of bondage. The mood in the Garden was strained. My men, sensing my concern, were sharp and the Pharisees were slowly backing away like scared little rabbits, unsure when to run and hide. The look in Jesus' eyes, the look of that lion, told me we tied Him up only because He allowed it. His look was one that said, 'You have no power over me.' As the coming hours would reveal, even His eyes spoke the truth."

CHAPTER 4

The Trials

I commented to Octavian that the arrest in the Garden was pretty intense. He said it was very intense but that everything eased now that they had Jesus under arrest. He then said that he was instructed by one of the religious leaders to take Him to Annas' house. I interrupted Octavian and asked why they took Jesus there? He said, "I had no idea." He continued, "I didn't even know who Annas was at the time. I found out on the way there that he was once the High Priest and that he was also the father-in-law of Caiaphas, who was the current High Priest. Again, what a mockery! We had no business going to Annas' house, but from what I was told, Annas wanted to question Jesus about His teachings, and he also had questions about His disciples. I thought that was a bit odd. His disciples (at the time) didn't seem like much of a concern to me. They weren't even there. I protested this detour to Annas' house and told the Pharisees that our instructions were to deliver Jesus to Pilate, but they assured me that Pilate was aware of what they were doing and had given his approval. I really wasn't exactly sure on this point and definitely not in the mood to argue with these little men, so I went along with their wishes."

"When we arrived at Annas' house, he acted so pompous in all his robes and tassels and such, like he thought he was the judge of all humanity. We ushered Jesus in, where several Jewish elders, along with Annas, sat trying to look as stern and holy as possible. Jesus, on the other hand, didn't show much concern. I was trying to feign interest, but this was not at all what I had wanted to do on that particular evening. Annas then made some formal gestures with his hands, evidently wanting to silence everyone. *The great one is about to speak,* I thought to myself, then in a very strict and serious tone, Annas began questioning Jesus.

Jesus answered Annas' question with a question, which I noticed He did a lot throughout His trial. 'Why do you ask me?'[14] He said to Annas. Jesus went on to say that He taught openly and in public and that what He said was no secret. He also mentioned to Annas that he should call in those who listened to Him. One of the Pharisees nearest to Jesus took this as disrespectful, and so he slapped Jesus in the face, and again, Jesus responded with a question. 'If I said something wrong, testify as to what is wrong. But if I spoke the truth, why

---

[14] John 18:21 (ESV).

did you strike me?"[15] I was tiring pretty quickly with the Pharisees, but little did I know they were just getting started on Jesus."

I asked Octavian how long they were at Annas' house. He said, "Not long, in fact, after Jesus was slapped and then asked the man who hit him to testify against His words, Annas seemed to squirm in his seat, like he was searching for something else to say. Everyone was looking at Annas, waiting for his response, but he was having trouble making eye contact with anyone. Annas, no doubt feeling the stares, acted as if he was so offended by Jesus and was done with Him. We were then instructed to take Jesus to Caiaphas, where He was to be asked more questions by the Sanhedrin. I then had one of my men grab Jesus by the arm, and we led Him to Caiaphas' chambers."

"At this trial, they, the Pharisees, and the elders of Israel had assembled and were all shouting one thing after another, accusing Him of this and that. All their arguments had to do with their laws and His false teachings, which opposed the laws of Moses. I was a little embarrassed for those poor little old men. They were acting like children. Jesus just stood silently, unaffected by their ranting and raving."

"The elders called up witness after witness, but they couldn't seem to get their stories straight. None of it, or

---

[15] John 18:23 (NIV).

them, seemed credible. My soldiers and I watched the proceedings, trying to follow along with what was going on. It was a confused and chaotic mockery of justice, but we had our orders and were following along like good soldiers."

"After a short while of berating and seething and punching Jesus, Caiaphas, the high priest, finally asked Him a direct question. His answer was chilling. The High Priest charged Him under oath by their God, to tell them if He was the Christ, the Son of God. Jesus firmly and without hesitation, said, 'It is as you say.'[16] My goodness did all hell break loose when Jesus said this; it was like a wave of evil rushed over the place. They all started shouting, 'He is worthy of death!'[17] Others started spitting on Jesus, hitting and mocking Him. For a bunch of holy men of God, they sure had a lot of hate and evil in them."

"This was not that surprising to any of us soldiers. We had seen the Pharisees in action for years and had a pretty good understanding of what was really inside of them. To be completely fair and honest, some of my soldiers joined in on the action. You know, for a brief moment, I caught a very unusual expression on the face of Jesus. I looked directly at Him as they were screaming, spitting, and punching Him. As I've said before, He was

---

[16] Luke 23:3 (NKJV).
[17] Matthew 26:66 (NIV).

so cool and calm. There was absolutely no fear in His eyes—just a deep and painful understanding of what was really happening. He was actually quite extraordinary! Clearly, He was affected by what they were saying and doing. I don't know who could have taken that onslaught of violence and humiliation and not have been, but He wasn't getting angry like any normal person. He seemed sad, and not for Himself, but for them. This was just another indication that Jesus was a different man than anyone I had ever come across."

I asked Octavian at this point if this was when he started to believe that Jesus might be the Messiah. He said, "Not at all. At the time, I just felt Jesus was a decent man who made the wrong people angry—the Pharisees." He then said, "I had many dealings with the Pharisees from the time I was first stationed in Jerusalem. A lot of teachers and leaders made them mad. They didn't want anyone challenging or threatening their power."

Octavian continued, "It was early in the morning now, roosters could be heard in the distance, and all the chief priests and the elders of the people were finally tired of the whole ordeal, and so they came to the decision to put Jesus to death. So, at the orders of Caiaphas, I again had a soldier grab Jesus by the arm, and we led Him away to Pilate, the governor. I had never met the Governor before that day, but I had heard rumors that he did not like to be bothered in the early morning hours. Given that, he was not happy to see any of us, especially these Pharisees. He, like pretty much everyone in the world, didn't like them very much. Then, as if Pilate wasn't already irritated enough, the Pharisees said they could not enter the palace because they didn't want to be defiled. Pilate, visibly offended, came out to them. I found that odd. Why was Pilate placating these religious leaders? It was almost as if Pilate was trying to please them."

"Being the Centurion on duty, Pilate gave me a very disapproving look, as if this were all my doing. All I could do was shrug. I knew he was upset, but it wasn't my fault. The Pharisees were a headache to every Roman I knew. All they did was shout a lot and point their bony little fingers at everyone who didn't meet their precious standards. My soldiers and I don't shout much at all. Why shout when the thrust of a sword is so much more effective? Trust me; I sure wanted to draw mine several times that day. At this point, Jesus was standing before Pilate, and he looked Him over and said to the Pharisees, something to the effect of, 'Why are you involving me in this matter?' One of the Pharisees told Pilate, Jesus was a criminal and that he needed to do something about it. Pilate shot back, 'Take Him yourselves and judge Him by your own law.'[18] But the Pharisees speaking with Pilate insisted that they had no au-

---
[18] John 18:31 (NIV).

thority to execute anyone. They were also shouting that He was a blasphemer and that according to their law, He was worthy of death. Jesus did not respond to them or even acknowledge their words. Pilate asked Jesus if He was going to say something in His defense, but Jesus said nothing, to Pilate's amazement."[19]

"Pilate told Jesus to follow him inside the palace so he could speak with Him. Ordering my men to stand guard between the palace and the religious leaders, I followed them because a man under arrest should not be alone with the Governor. Once inside, Pilate asked Jesus if He was the King of the Jews. Again, Jesus answered Pilate's question with a question, 'Is that your own idea, or did others talk to you about me?'[20] Pilate answered, 'Am I a Jew?' Jesus responded that His kingdom was not of this world but from another place.[21] Pilate sarcastically responded, 'You are a King, then!'[22] Jesus answered, 'You say that I am a king.'[23] Jesus also told Pilate that He came to testify to the truth. Pilate just shook his head and said, 'What is truth?'[24] Pilate then went back out to the religious leaders and said, 'I find no basis for a charge against Him.'"[25]

---

[19] Matthew 27:14.

[20] John 18:34 (NIV).

[21] John 18:36.

[22] John 18:37 (NIV).

[23] John 18:37 (NIV).

[24] John 18:38 (NIV).

[25] Ibid.

I raised a hand and motioned for Octavian to hold for a minute. I was writing everything he was saying as fast as I could and wanted to make sure I had everything correct up to that point. I read back to him a couple of paragraphs, and he nodded. "That is correct." I then asked Octavian what he was thinking about with all that was happening. He said he was a little confused but that he still didn't find Jesus to be a sympathetic figure, just some guy the Pharisees hated. Octavian went on to say, "Pilate, clearly frustrated by the Pharisees, told me to take Jesus and have Him flogged. Again, I ordered a soldier to grab Jesus by the arm, and we led Him away to the Praetorium to be whipped. Jesus didn't put up any kind of protest or fight. He just submitted to the soldier and walked peacefully beside him. I remember thinking, *Well, at least He is cooperating*. It was there that some of my men were a little rough with Jesus. He was beaten, mocked, and they shoved Him around a bit. Then we led Jesus back to Pilate."

"Pilate went out to the religious leaders, huddled up like a pack of snarling hyenas, and again said, 'I find no basis for a charge against him.'[26] The religious leaders started shouting, He must die.[27] Pilate tried to reason with them that Jesus did not deserve death, but again they shouted back, 'According to that law He must

---

[26] John 19:4 (NIV).
[27] John 19:6.

die, because He claimed to be the Son of God.'[28] This was when everything took a dramatic turn. Pilate was shocked by this statement and shot a look at Jesus, but Jesus stood silently unmoved and undaunted. I know I have mentioned this before, but Jesus and His demeanor throughout this whole process were astounding. He didn't flinch when being struck, He didn't whimper or cry, as many do, He didn't even try to defend Himself. With all this abuse and the accusations flying, not a sound from Him could be heard."

"Because of the statement that Jesus claimed to be the Son of God, Pilate motioned for me to bring Jesus back inside where he asked Him, 'Where do you come from?'[29] Jesus said nothing. Pilate then said, 'Don't you realize I have the power to either free you or to crucify you?'[30] Jesus looked straight at Pilate and said, 'You... have no power over me.'[31] I could see the lion in Jesus' eyes again. Pilate must have seen it, too, because he looked a bit unsettled by His gaze. Not knowing what to say, Pilate looked down and motioned for us to follow him, and so I grabbed Jesus and led Him back outside to the Pharisees where Pilate again tried to release Jesus."

"It seemed the religious leaders decided to change their tactics because now they were shouting Jesus

---

[28] John 19:7 (NIV).
[29] John 19:9 (NIV).
[30] John 19:10 (NIV).
[31] John 19:11 (NIV).

claimed to be their King, and in doing so, opposed Caesar.[32] The implication of this new charge was that Jesus was in rebellion against Rome and, therefore, an insurrectionist who had to be punished by Pilate. Punishment for insurrection was crucifixion. Then one of the Pharisees yelled that Jesus was stirring everyone up against Caesar and Rome and that He began in Galilee and has come all the way here. Pilate seemed to jump at this statement and asked if Jesus was a Galilean.[33] When this was confirmed, Pilate acted relieved because, as a Galilean, Jesus would have been under Herod's jurisdiction. With this new information, Pilate ordered us to take Jesus before Herod. I think Pilate was hoping Herod would take this responsibility off his hands and make a decision. Pilate didn't want to deal with the problem, and so he did what leaders often do, pass it on to someone else."

I asked Octavian if he knew Herod or if this was his first encounter with him. He said he knew who all the Governors were but, like Pilate, had never met him before that day. I then asked Octavian what happened at Herod's palace. He said, "Herod was giddy when we arrived there like he was someone important because Pilate needed his help. Immediately, I was disgusted by this fat little man, but I dared not show it. Power does

---

[32] John 19:12.
[33] Luke 23:5-6.

not like to be showed up. Herod also seemed to relish the idea of meeting Jesus. He must have heard of Jesus' miraculous powers because Herod was trying to get Him to do some 'magic tricks,' but Jesus just ignored Him.[34] Herod asked Jesus a few questions, but He did not even respond. I snickered under my breath because Jesus wouldn't even look Herod in the eyes. I can't imagine what Herod would have done had Jesus turned His intimidating gaze on him. He probably would have wet himself. The fact that Jesus did not look at Herod must have embarrassed him because he and his council started to mock and ridicule Jesus. Then they put a robe on Him and were mocking Him as a King. Herod then made a show for his guests that he didn't want to be bothered anymore with this criminal and told us to take Him back to Pilate. You know I heard Herod died a pretty horrible death very recently. It seems, from what I heard, he was being praised as some 'god' and then fell ill to a disease of the gut.[35] I wondered after hearing this how anyone could foolishly think they were divine after meeting Jesus?" I said that I had heard Herod died as well, and to really no one's regret.

Octavian continued, "After our short march from Herod's place, we were back at the Palace, but Pilate had moved to Gabbatha—the judge's seat, so we took Him

---

[34] Luke 23:8-9.
[35] Acts 12:21-23.

there. When we brought Jesus out to Pilate, he immediately shot me a... 'You are in so much trouble when this is over,' look. I didn't know what to say; it was the Pharisees. They had the whole town stirred up over Jesus. All I was doing was following his orders. But I didn't dare say anything in my defense because Pilate was getting really mad now. As I have reflected on this day, it is kind of funny now, certainly not at the time, though, but with all of Rome's power and prestige, the Governor was not in charge of this hearing. Oh, Pilate tried to act like he was in control, but he wasn't, and the Pharisees were trying to control the proceedings, but they couldn't. Jesus was the only one who had any self-control, and they all knew it. The only one who was really free was the prisoner. This made no sense to me. How had Pilate allowed it to get this far? All he had to do was tell the Pharisees to be gone, and it would have ended. Sadly, Pilate appeared powerless to do so. You know, I lost a lot of respect for Pilate that day. He wasn't being a leader at all. Those Jewish leaders were one step ahead of Pilate, along with the rest of us. Clearly, they had planned this all out. We were simply reacting to their moves. I know the Pharisees are their religious leaders, and some of them may be good ones, but really they act more like politicians. Always working the angles, fighting for their power, and showing little concern for their people. Much like our Roman Senate, in all honesty."

"Minutes after bringing Jesus before Pilate at Gabbatha, something strange happened. A servant interrupted the trial because he needed to deliver Pilate a message from his wife. I couldn't hear what the servant said, but Pilate's mood quickly changed. Man, I tell you, Pilate looked absolutely shaken—like he had just seen a ghost! I found out later (rumors spread fast in the palace) that Pilate's wife had some frightening dreams about Jesus and told her husband not to have anything to do with that righteous man.[36] After hearing the message, Pilate tried to argue with the mob and the Pharisees. The whole trial was unraveling now. Pilate lost control; the crowd was in a frenzy, along with the Pharisees, who were like rabid dogs, growling with bared teeth. Seeing all this madness, I shot a glance at Jesus, standing there, right out in the middle of it all. His head was tilted up, and I think He was praying because His lips were moving a little. I was so impressed by His character. I see this scene in my mind from time to time, and I have to smile about it now, what Jesus knew at that moment that none of us did. It was obvious the Pharisees had their plan, but from the look on Jesus' face, He knew His father in Heaven had His plan too."

I stopped Octavian at this point and told him again how thankful I was for his insights. He said it was his honor. I then asked, "What happened after this?"

---

[36] Matthew 27:19.

"Pilate was vexed and getting madder by the minute. The crowd, now spurred on by the Pharisees, started shouting 'Crucify, Crucify.'[37] Pilate saw no reason for handing Jesus over to be crucified."

"What did you think?" I asked Octavian. He said, "Though I had been indifferent to Jesus before, I was now convinced Jesus had done nothing worthy of death." He then said to me, "You asked before if I had started to believe that Jesus just may be the Messiah and I had said 'no.' Well, it was at this moment, I started to wonder. There were just too many things about Jesus' behavior and attitude that were not like any normal human being. The other thing I knew was, Jesus had real power and authority like I'd never seen before. In retrospect, I believe this was why the Pharisees were so mad at Jesus. They were jealous of Him. Do you know what I find sad and satisfying all at the same time? Watching power squirm. I say this because I believe both Pilate and the Pharisees knew Jesus had true authority, and they did not. Pilate also knew Jesus was different from any of the other men he had tried before because of the charges being brought by the religious leaders and by the dreams his wife had. I have been to Gabbatha, the Judge's seat, many times guarding prisoners, and I had never seen Pilate behave the way he did with Jesus. It was a little uncomfortable watching someone with the

---

[37] John 19:15.

power of Rome behind him, being stripped of it right before my very eyes. I imagine that is what Jesus did to a lot of powerful people. I know that is what happened to me in the Garden when I was hurled to the ground at the sound of His voice. I should have known then, in the Garden. Pilate should have known as well. This man was the Son of God! You know, I see things so much differently after that day. Man's power is one of them. Man does have power and can hold it over other men's heads, but God is the only one with true power and authority. As I told you, these were the hours that changed my life."

I mused at how wise Octavian was and told him so. He flatly rejected my compliment and said if not for Jesus, he would not be wise at all. And there his wisdom was shining through again. Then I asked him to proceed...

"Pilate offered to release Jesus, as was the governor's custom during the feast. He thought maybe they would allow him (I can't believe how I am saying this, Pilate was the Governor after all) to have Jesus flogged again and then discharged, but all the people started shouting that they wanted Pilate to release Barabbas.[38] When I heard this, I was shocked. Barabbas was a known insurrectionist and murderer. How could Pilate even consider releasing this criminal? Was there no justice in Rome? To think Pilate was going to condemn this righteous

---

[38] Mark 15:6-11.

man and set a known murderer free was unacceptable! This day continued to get stranger and stranger. Little did I know that the hours that were to follow would top any I could ever have imagined."

"Pilate finally gave up or gave in, I should say. He did something interesting and, in my opinion, quite cowardly. He made a big show to the crowd by taking a bowl of water and then washing his hands of the whole mess. 'I am innocent of this man's blood!' he shouted.[39] As I have come to learn, none of us are innocent of Jesus' blood. We all, by our actions, put Jesus on the cross. Pilate then said something bizarre. He said to the mob that had formed at Gabbatha, 'Here is your King!'[40] I raised my eyebrows in shock. What was Pilate doing now? Had he come to the conclusion Jesus truly was a King? Or was he trying to goad the crowd? I'm not sure which it was, but one thing I am certain of, the crowd erupted. They were screaming loudly and started to push forward. Thinking the mob might rush the Governor, I drew my sword as I quickly moved between the crowd and Pilate. The rattle of clanging steel echoed across the stone pavement as my men drew their swords and formed a line of defense behind me. The crowd backed only slightly, which started my blood to boil. How dare they challenge our steel. Pilate, startled

---

[39] Matthew 17:24 (NIV).
[40] John 19:5 (NIV); John 19:13 (NIV).

by the crowd and the sounds of our swords, hurriedly gave the order to release Barabbas, the one they asked for, and surrendered Jesus to their will."

"The Governor commanded us to take Jesus away to be flogged and crucified. Without taking my eyes off the crowd, I slowly started to back away and ordered my men to escort Jesus to the Praetorium. We wanted out of there as fast as we could, hoping that removing Jesus would settle the crowd, which it seemed to do." On our way to the grounds behind the palace, which was near our barracks, Jesus again looked at me. I was puzzled because He appeared to give me a nod of appreciation. Like He was proud of the way I handled that situation. I know it sounds odd, but that is exactly what I felt He communicated with me. He confirmed to me later that He indeed was proud of me."

I stopped him right there and raised my voice a little. I said, "He confirmed with you later? What do you mean by that?" Octavian just smiled and said, "In due time, Justus, in due time." Shaking my head in confusion, I said, in a pouting sort of way, "Fine." Then Octavian said a little sternly, "May I continue? Because what I am about to tell you is quite difficult." I straightened up in my chair, apologized, and said, "Continue."

"It was here, at our soldier's barracks, that the power of Rome was unleashed on Jesus. However, it was not just Rome's power, as I would later learn, it was the powers of Hell."

Octavian then turned his head away and pushed his chair back from the table. I asked him if he was alright. He said nothing except, "I'll be back," in a very short and curt manner, and then briskly walked away. I noticed him falter a bit, and even though I didn't have a clear idea what was wrong, this tough Centurion was visibly moved. I didn't think I had offended him, but I did suspect he left because I thought I saw his eyes tear up, and maybe he was embarrassed and didn't want to show any weakness. I also thought that he might have needed a break. I know I needed one too because my writing hand was stiffening. As I would discover after a few moments, we both needed this break more than I could have known. For what Octavian was about to relay to me were some of the most difficult things I had, and would, ever hear. I can't even imagine what it was like for Octavian to have witnessed what he was about to tell me.

CHAPTER 5

The Praetorium

I was sitting at the table trying to rest my mind while rubbing and stretching my writing hand when Mary of Clopas walked up carrying a pitcher of water and two cups and said, "I thought you both might be needing something to drink." I was very grateful. I had been so focused on everything Octavian was saying that I didn't realize how thirsty I was and figured Octavian must be just as thirsty. Mary asked how everything was going, and I told her it was going great but that we were taking a little break. We chatted for a moment, and then Octavian came into view, making his way over to us. I have to admit; I was relieved to see him approaching. I had concerns he may not return. When he reached us, he looked a bit more composed, and embracing Mary, he noticed the pitcher of water. He thanked her for bringing it over, and as he was sitting down, I poured him a cup. Mary smiled and said, "Well, I'd better be off."

As she walked away, Octavian shook his head and said, "The followers of Jesus are so warm and kind. I've never felt this kind of love and acceptance before, and without doing anything to deserve it. I have felt the respect of my commanding officers on the battlefield and certainly the respect of my soldiers under me. Respect is good, and I absolutely want to be respected, but love is different. With love, true love, like the love of Jesus, you don't have to earn it. You can only receive it. Respect is earned, but love is a gift. This is one of the reasons I feel at peace with the followers of Jesus, Jewish or not. I feel as though they truly love me."

Octavian adjusted his seat and moved a bit closer. Something in his mood had changed. I furrowed my brow, wondering what this meant. I hoped the evening wasn't coming to a close. There was so much more I wanted to know. Octavian, with a very serious look on his face, leaned forward and said in lowered tones that what he was about to tell me he had never spoken of in detail to anyone and that he was not proud of his actions, but it needed to be recorded none the less. He apologized again for what he was about to say, and I could sense his shame, but I reminded him of the loving ways of Jesus and His followers. Octavian managed a slight smile and then proceeded.

"As I had said, Pilate ordered us to take Jesus away to the Praetorium to be flogged and crucified. On our way there, even though it was still in the morning, the sun was already getting hot. The day was going to be a scorcher. It had been a long night, and my detachment and I were pretty tired. I knew from the look on His face that Jesus was also very tired. Since His arrest at Gethsemane, Jesus had not been allowed to sit, rest, eat, or drink. Like I said before, there were no complaints or whining from Him. He took it all with such unbelievable grace. We had arrested Jesus in what seemed like an eternity ago, and then throughout the night, went from one place to another and saw one ruler after another. None of them had answers—only questions and accusations. Could it be that the one with all the answers was the One on trial? I have learned this, after those long hours by Jesus' side, mankind, from the least to the greatest, is a weak, flawed, and an insecure lot. One moment spent with Jesus revealed this great contrast and a vast chasm between God and humans."

Again, I could see and hear the wisdom of this aging Centurion. He went on, "When we entered the Praetorium, something definitely changed." Octavian became quiet for a moment and looked upward, as if to heaven, and muttered something under his breath. Then he continued...

"It was kind of eerie. Soldiers from other Cohorts, who had not even been a part of the long night's proceedings, were coming out of the barracks, not just to see what was going on but to get in on what was starting to take place. This was another unusual site, for rarely, if ever, have I seen this kind of interest over a prisoner about to be flogged. Floggings were such a regular occurrence, and so I wondered what the fascination was now. But here they were, a crowd of Romans soldiers—more like a pack of wild dogs. Or more accurately, the 'Bulls of Bashan,' as your King David wrote.[41] Octavian appeared to drift away for a moment as I sat intensely watching him. "I love hearing the Psalms read," he finally said. "They are so comforting. I also like that they are the writings of such a brave warrior. The world cannot have enough of them."

Octavian shook his head and sort of came back to the present. I wondered if again he needed a little respite from what he was recalling. He went on to say, "This was when a hellish frenzy broke loose. I have to admit, I completely lost control of my men and myself, for that matter. The whole Praetorium turned into a sporting arena. I really can't explain why everything, or should I say, everyone, grew so out of control. It makes no sense in the natural. We had flogged and beaten many prisoners in my time of service as a Roman Centurion. It was a normal function of the Praetorium guard, but this time it was very different. I've never seen such, and I don't know how else to describe it, such an "evil glee" in my cohort and the soldiers under my fellow Centurions. As I said earlier, everyone in the Praetorium guard had

---

[41] Psalms 22:12 (NIV).

heard of or had seen Jesus, and many held Him in high regard. However, now everyone was eager to get their hands on Him. I'm ashamed to admit it, but even I went from being fairly indifferent toward Jesus to actually joining in and enjoying the frantic madness. I understand now, as I am growing in my knowledge and faith of spiritual things, that the origin of this madness was from the pit of hell, breaking loose on Jesus. It was almost as if the devil knew what Jesus was going to do on that cross, and he was trying to stop Him by killing Him through us in the Praetorium. The soldiers around me became hell's accomplices, and so did I. But it wouldn't work. Any normal human would have died from the beating we doled out on Jesus, but He just took it all. I can't explain how He physically survived. He was drawing on a strength I had never witnessed in a man."

"The whole company of soldiers was gathered around Jesus, taunting, punching, and kicking Him. I can't tell you how many times He was knocked down and either got up under His own strength or was picked up by a soldier. On and on, this went. Jesus was being pushed and shoved all over the grounds as my men made sport of Him. His clothes were ripped off, and one of the soldiers wove a crown of thorns and smashed it on His head. Another soldier draped a scarlet robe over Him and put a staff in His hand. Everyone was laughing at and mocking Him as a "King".[42] Other soldiers were bowing down before Him only to rise to their feet to hit Him again. I will never forget that day, though I have tried many times."

Octavian looked down, shaking his head in shame, recalling what had happened, and then he looked up at me. I slowly let out a breath and then stifled the urge to say something helpful or encouraging to Octavian because I could see the look of anguish on his face. Instead, the seriousness in his eyes told me to hold my tongue and listen. During our short time together, I had become fairly comfortable with Octavian and felt like we were becoming friends. He was now my brother in the Lord and not some feared Centurion like I felt when I first saw him, but now, Now the Centurion was back and sitting right in front of me. I was slightly afraid for the first time since our introduction. Seeing the look in the Centurion's eyes, I felt a little panic rising in my chest. He must have been getting angry because the scar under his eye that stretched to the bridge of his nose was becoming even more pronounced. All of a sudden, as if sent by Jesus Himself, John appeared out of nowhere at the table and gently put his hand on Octavian's shoulder. Octavian, deep in thought-like trance, was startled and shot a menacing glance upward, but after seeing it was John, relaxed. Whew, I breathed a

---

[42] John 19:2-3.

sigh of relief. With John's presence, all the stress and anxiety I was feeling at the table evaporated. Thanks be to God for His intervention through Brother John.

Octavian gave John a nod, and a faint smile formed on his lips. I could see the two had a special bond that only those who have gone through a tragedy shared. As John walked away, Octavian turned back to me and said, "Where were we?" I cautiously reminded him he was telling me about the flogging and the Praetorium.

"That's right, as I had said, floggings were commonplace for criminals, especially one who was charged with insurrection against Rome. In fact, it was mandatory. Rome would not stand for any sedition. This time, the beating of Jesus was not normal. This was different. The soldiers were possessed by something outside of themselves. At the time, I could not explain it, but now, I am certain we were possessed by the demons of Hell."

"One of the soldiers then ripped the blood-soaked robe off of Jesus, and the actual flogging began. The soldier assigned to this task used a flagrum, which is a whip made of leather straps that have metal and glass attached at the ends. These straps would tear at the flesh of a man, opening him up. Blood was now flowing from every part of Jesus. The flogging became more and more intense as the soldiers laughed and shouted. I knew things were getting out of hand, and shamefully, I could not stop it. Order and decorum were gone, just like what had happened with Pilate. I guess I lost a little respect for myself that day as well in all of the frenzy."

"Jesus looked right at me at this moment during the flogging. I think about that a lot now. Numerous times our eyes would meet, from the arrest to the trial, here at the Praetorium and then on the cross—at almost every juncture of the night and day. I know part of the reason was my proximity to the whole proceedings, but it was more than that. It was almost as if He was saying something to me through those brilliant eyes. I felt like they were saying, 'You know you belong to me,' and the look of compassion toward myself and everyone involved is something even some of my soldiers have mentioned. I would love for everyone in the world to see His eyes and know the way He views them. Without a doubt, it would change them too. When we were at our very worst, He still loved us.[43] That is why I stated before that when I have fears or doubts, I think about His eyes and the way He looked at me like no other has ever seen me."

"When Jesus looked at me during the flogging, as I was watching and laughing, along with everyone else, something happened to me. His eyes brought me to my senses because I immediately felt shame over what was taking place and how it was being done. I looked around at the whole scene, and then rage came over me. I screamed at the top of my lungs, 'ENOUGH!' but

[43] Romans 5:8.

a number of soldiers continued to laugh and mock, and the man flogging Jesus struck another blow. Furious they did not heed my command, I drew my sword from its scabbard and made a move toward them, again shouting 'ENOUGH!' Immediately two other Centurions, my brothers on the battlefield, were at my side, swords drawn as well. A Centurion must never draw a sword alone—all Centurions know this. If one draws his weapon, we all must. We have to have each other's back. Felix and Ignatius covered my blind spots as we faced off with this group of possessed soldiers. Immediately the soldiers started to back away. We Centurions believe one hundred soldiers are no match for one of us. By the look on the soldier's faces, they believed it too."

This was so intense, I thought to myself. I looked up at Octavian because of the lull, and he appeared to be a little pale. I did not want to interrupt again, so I put my head back down and continued writing as he continued speaking.

"Everywhere around the Praetorium, everything and everyone became very quiet. You could smell the sweat and blood in the air. Jesus, on the ground, was slowly and painfully trying to pull Himself to His feet. I commanded a soldier nearest to Jesus to help Him up. I then ordered all the soldiers who were not in my detachment back to their barracks. Turning to my brother Centurions, Felix and Ignatius, I thanked them for coming to my side."

"Next, I told the men in my detachment to put the crossbar on Jesus' shoulders and lead Him away to Golgotha, also known as the place of the Skull, to be crucified."[44]

"Jesus was so exhausted and weak from the loss of blood that we were having a difficult time making progress. He kept falling and struggling to get up. It was at this moment I began to feel sorry for Jesus. This was a new sensation for me, for I had never felt any compassion for a criminal, especially one charged with insurrection, but now I couldn't help myself. It was like the whole weight of the world, not just the cross, was on His shoulders, and He was not going to quit. He was an impressive man to take all that He did and still keep fighting. I couldn't even fathom, at that moment, how He remained conscious. I don't know what came over me, but I felt a sense of amazement as I watched Jesus struggle for every step. He was so determined to finish the ordeal."

"Then, out of nowhere, and I can't explain why, but I felt a fury rise from within me. It was like an anger I could taste. Whether it was out of haste, frustration, shame, or seeing all that had transpired, I became very angry. I was angry with the Pharisees, angry with Pi-

---

[44] John 19:17.

THE HOURS THAT CHANGED MY LIFE

late, and with the soldiers back at the Praetorium. I was even angry with the mob that was following us and getting in our way. With all of the people, the noise, the blood and sweat, and the fatigue, I was losing control. Seeing Jesus struggling and wanting it all to be over, I even felt anger toward Him. *Why wasn't He dead already?* I snarled to myself. Any other man would have been, given the beating He received. If He had died on the grounds of the Praetorium, this whole thing would be over by now. I was angry and getting angrier with each step and stumble Jesus took. I wanted Him to hurry up so we could finish our duty and be done with it all."

"There have been times in my life when I could get so angry that everyone close to me was in danger. I had been known to fly into such a rage that I would totally lose all self-control. That served me well on the battlefield but scarcely anywhere else. I could feel that kind of uncontrollable rage rising in my chest at that moment, but I could not lose control here on this busy street with so many in the crowd. So I grabbed one of them, an onlooker, a man I later learned was named Simon of Cyrene, and forced him to carry the cross.[45] On a normal day, there may have been some protest from a civilian with an order like this from a Roman, but when Simon saw the look in my eyes, he complied right away and lifted the cross from Jesus' shoulders and proceeded to

---

[45] Matthew 27:32.

carry the cross without a word. With the crossbar lifted, Jesus' face, covered in mud and blood, turned upward, and looking straight at me, mouthed what I thought were the words, 'Thank you.' Like an arrow that pierced my heart, all the anger seemed to leave me, and I felt a calm and peace wash over me. His unexpected compassion and kindness completely defused my rage. Overwhelmed by His gesture, as I was bending down to help Him to His feet, I said in a low voice, so as not to be heard by my soldiers, 'You're welcome.' I passed Jesus off to two of my soldiers and told them to assist Him the rest of the way."

I raised my hand, and Octavian tilted his head curiously. I thought for a moment and questioned within myself whether or not to ask Octavian another question, and before I was through with my inner debate, I blurted out, "Why didn't you want your soldiers to hear you speaking to Jesus?" "Well, for one thing," he said, "I did not want my men to see or hear any compassion coming from me toward a prisoner. It sets a bad precedence. I would not want them to feel sorry for a criminal on the way to a crucifixion, but just to do their job. I did not care so much if they showed hostility, but never compassion, and especially not for one charged with insurrection, as was Jesus. We Centurions try to take emotions out of our duty—It is the Roman Legion's way. The other reason is we do not have conversations of any kind with criminals. We use force and our steel, but not our words. If you were under my arrest, I would not ask you to do something, nor would I tell you. I would make you do what I wanted. This, in and of itself, communicates to you that your wishes, feelings, or pain are none of my concern. We Centurions use our silence and indifference to intimidate criminals into submission. I also do not care what they have to say. I ignore them completely. That is until this particular crucifixion. Who Jesus was and what He said became all too important to me." All I could muster after Octavian's explanation was, "Oh." Now I felt a little dumb for blurting out the question, but thankfully, Octavian didn't seem too bothered and continued...

"With Jesus being assisted, we were now moving at a better pace, but we still had to push through the crowd, which slowed us a little. This, too, was unusual, as so many things were during those long hours that changed my life. Normally when we took a criminal to the Skull, there may be a small group of family and friends. More often than not, there was no one around, and certainly never a crowd. Crucifixions were just too gory for most people to stomach. Today, however, there were a lot of onlookers and a diverse lot at that. Some were just curious bystanders; others, like the religious leaders and their followers, were foaming and frothing hate-filled words at Jesus. One of the Pharisees attempted to spit at Jesus but accidentally hit one of my men. Punched to the ground, my soldier stood over that Pharisee as my other soldiers reached for their swords. The Pharisees backed up, along with the rest of the crowd. As they were helping their wobbly religious leader to his feet, I wondered if he would ever spit at someone again. The fact that he was missing a couple of teeth would have made that more difficult. In the crowd were also some women following Jesus who were weeping as they watched."

"By the time we reached Golgotha, all of us were tired, sweaty, and dirty. However, only one of us was bloody. There were two other criminals who we crucified that day. I didn't know who they were or even why they were being crucified. I didn't care. One of my men said the two criminals were thieves and that they were companions of Barabbas. Pilate ordered them to be taken away to the 'Skull' in place of Barabbas. I think Pilate did this because he was embarrassed over having to release Barabbas instead of Jesus. I just shrugged my shoulders and thought, who cared who was being crucified with Jesus? He was the only one that mattered. One of the two we placed on Jesus' right and the other on His left."[46]

---

[46] Matthew 27:38.

CHAPTER 6

The Cross

Octavian paused a moment, and I seized the opportunity in the lull to again thank him for sharing what must have been something so horrible to have experienced. He nodded in agreement and said, "I don't think I have said this many words in one sitting my entire life. In my line of work, I do not have a lot of conversations with people." He then thanked me for writing it all down for the record. "People have to know what Jesus did for them on the cross. It must never be forgotten. I hope this helps the followers of Jesus in the Decapolis." I told Octavian, "I think they are going to be very thankful for what you have spoken about here tonight. I also think they will love Jesus more and more for all He did for them. My prayer is that your account of all that happened in those hours that changed you helps the whole world know Jesus better. I hope they see Him through your eyes." Octavian had a grateful and satisfied look on his face. The satisfied look of a soldier carrying out his mission.

Octavian sighed deeply as if gathering himself for what came next. I looked at him with my quill, ready to write. He began, "Exhausted from everything that had happened since the arrest and with the overhead sun beating down on us, we began to prepare Jesus and the two criminals for crucifixion. The two others to be crucified were cursing and twisting their bodies in a struggle to free themselves from my soldiers. They were screaming and pleading for us to stop. One of my soldiers punched one of them in the gut to shut him up and calm him down. Two more of my men held his arms down so he could be nailed to the cross. Jesus, on the other hand, was surprisingly cooperative. He didn't fight or struggle with them, which was odd. He was even courteous toward my soldiers and asked them how they preferred Him on the cross. When they told Him what they wanted Him to do and began helping Him into position, He actually thanked them. There was no hesitation from Jesus whatsoever, which was very unusual for someone about to be crucified. He had completely surrendered Himself to the process, which confused the soldiers. My men, having crucified many people, are very familiar with this job and know what must be done and in what order, but the way Jesus handled everything with such grace, well, He threw everything off. Jesus was actually making us re-think all our duties."

"How do you mean?" I interjected. "Well, one example," Octavian said, "When the soldiers started to affix Jesus to the cross, they were confused because Jesus put His own hands and feet where they needed to be placed. This caused the soldiers to look at each other and then at me in disbelief and confusion. Jesus was throwing our rhythms and timing off. None of our duties that day had their usual, natural flow. We had to think about our duties because everything was out of the ordinary. I believe this is one of the reasons it is easy for me to remember the events of that day." "That makes sense," I said. "It's amazing how grace can throw us all off a bit. It must be because it is so unexpected."

Octavian then said, "Make no mistake though; amid all His courtesy and grace, you could still see that old familiar look in Jesus' eyes—those of a lion. It was also similar to the look I had seen on the battlefield as soldiers prepare themselves for a charge they know they may not survive—a stare of steel and determination for what lies before them. Many times I have seen fear in the eyes of soldiers, but there are those who, like Jesus, have a look of defiance toward the enemy. I respect those men more than any ruler. We would have fewer wars if the rich and ruling class had to face their enemies and not some lowly soldier. My respect for Jesus continued to grow. If only those pathetic Pharisees who were sneering at Him could see what real power and grace is—He was right before me, on a cross. The King of the Jews, choosing to fight for His people and not a low-ranking warrior forced into battle."

I stopped Octavian at this and said, "You just called Jesus the 'King of the Jews. Was it at this time you started to believe that Jesus was the Messiah?" He sat back and thought for a moment, "I think so, now that you put it that way. I can't explain it. The way Jesus responded to everything kept telling me He was different, that He was good."

Octavian continued, "Naturally, the other two who were being crucified were doing what every person I have crucified has done. They struggled, begged, or pleaded with all their might for us to stop or wait. It is very frightening to feel the cold steel of a seven-inch spike on your feet and wrists and then to see the hammer descending. To be honest with you, I've seen many Roman soldiers get a little weak in the knees at the sight. Of course, they would all deny it for the teasing they would receive from other soldiers. I have had to look away many times. This part of the crucifixion is the part I hate the most. I started to turn my head away as the hammer came down on the one thief, and I caught Jesus' eyes, again looking right at me, and then toward the thief as he let out an excruciating scream. Jesus' look sort of reassured me that it was alright, that everything must happen this way. I am sure Jesus felt sorry for the thief and me."

I told Octavian how fascinating and also how horrible this must have been to witness. I went on to say, "You hear about how Jesus died on the cross for your sins, and you are very grateful and moved by His love for you and the whole world, but as you are describing it, I get a different sense of it all. It was not glamorous or neatly packaged and tied with a bow. It was dirty, smelly, bloody, loud, and chaotic." Octavian said, "If you have never seen a crucifixion, consider yourself fortunate. They are the worst form of death. And the flogging and the beating of Jesus only added to His suffering on the cross. I still can't believe He lived as long as He did because the blood loss alone was unhuman. Peter has said before that Jesus shed His blood for our sins. This I know is true. I also know there must have been a lot of sins to pay for."[47]

Wanting to get us back on track, I asked Octavian why they used nails. I said I had seen a crucifixion once before, but they used leather straps to hold the arms and feet. "Sure," he said, "We didn't always use nails to affix a criminal to a cross. Like you said, sometimes we use leather straps or ropes. It just depended on the criminal, the crime committed, or the mood of the Centurion overseeing the crucifixion. Obviously, nails

---

[47] 1 Peter 1:18-19.

were the worst way for a person to be crucified. The use of nails sped up the process because of the additional blood loss. Those crucified for treason against Rome were treated in the most merciless way, with no quarter given. Since Jesus was convicted by Pilate for such a crime as treason, nails were the mandated choice."

"While the soldiers who were chosen began driving the nails into Jesus' wrists and ankles, I started to hammer a sign at the headpiece of the cross that read—'Jesus of Nazareth, King of the Jews.'[48] Pilate wanted this put there so the bystanders could read it and know what His crime was. I think he was also trying to show up the Pharisees because Pilate commanded that the sign be written in Aramaic, Latin, and Greek. This was not the usual practice, for the charges against a criminal were rarely, if ever, placed on the head of the cross, and then to have those charges written in three languages was unprecedented. Nevertheless, Pilate wanted everyone, including the Jews, to know that Jesus was the King of the Jews. The Pharisees were protesting the sign and wanted us to take it down altogether or to have it rewritten to say that Jesus only "claimed" to be their king.[49] I'll give it to Pilate on this one point; from what I heard, he stood his ground against those religious leaders and did not give in to their temper tantrums. Pilate

---

[48] John 19:19.
[49] John 19:21-22.

simply answered them, 'What is written, is written.'[50] Given these orders from Pilate, I ignored the Pharisees and hammered away."

"For some reason, while the nails were being driven into Jesus' wrists and ankles, four other soldiers started tearing at Jesus' clothing, each fighting to get a piece. The undergarment He was wearing was seamless, and not wanting to tear it, they cast lots to see who would win this prized possession.[51] There have been some rumors going around the barracks that I was the one who took the seamless undergarment, but I assure you, I do not have it, nor would I have wanted it. That whole affair of casting lots for His clothing was not something I took part in or approved of, and later I reprimanded the soldiers for the further shaming of Jesus. I know I had said earlier that I was indifferent to Jesus, but by this time, I was sick to my stomach and wanted it to be over. Many doubts crept into my head over what Pilate had commanded us to do. Could it be, I thought, that we were all wrong and Jesus was the only righteous one among us?"

"Another interesting thing that happened at this time is that one of the soldiers offered Jesus some wine mixed with an herb.[52] I believe it was myrrh. Often,

---

[50] John 19:22 (NIV).
[51] John 19:23-24.
[52] Matthew 27:34.

when men were crucified, there were some religious people who had compassion for the criminals. They kept this brew nearby, and it was given to criminals to help deaden the pain and dull their senses. Remarkably, Jesus, who must have been extremely thirsty, refused to drink any of it. As I have reflected on this moment and His refusal of the mixture, I have come to the conclusion that He did not want to be numb to any of the pain of the crucifixion. This was just one more instance of His composure and courage."

I broke in on Octavian and told him one of the disciples, who was teaching from the book of Psalms, spoke about this some time ago when I was here in Jerusalem. King David prophesied about this very event. "Ah, King David, my warrior friend. Well, his words were again proven true." He went on to say, "I am learning so much more about Jesus' crucifixion and all the prophecies in the Scriptures regarding His death. It is so amazing to me, and further proof, that Jesus is the Christ."

"After we hoisted the cross into place on Skull Hill, we stood back to watch. It was my duty, assigned by Rome, to oversee many crucifixions, something that I had become all too familiar with doing. Many people were there, which, again, was unusual. Normally at crucifixions, there were only a few people hanging around. Listen, you and I both know that crucifixions are horrible and can last for hours, so it was normal for the few who had concerns or feelings for the criminal to leave rather quickly. It was too unbearable and horrific to watch. I had learned to shut it off; you know, the cries and the moaning and all. I had become pretty much desensitized to the gruesome proceedings. But Jesus' crucifixion was different. As I said, many people were still gathered at the cross. Some were enjoying it in a grotesque sort of way, and others were weeping. One of the soldiers pointed out Mary, His mother. I couldn't believe she was there. Her son, Jesus, was almost unrecognizable. I would not have wanted my mother to see me that way. I was surprised that somebody hadn't taken her away. It was just that awful to watch. Then Jesus said something that was unlike anything I had ever heard from someone on a cross. He said, 'Father, forgive them, they do not know what they are doing.'[53] How often those words echo through my mind. You know, you hear a lot of things during a crucifixion as men are dying. Many plead for mercy, some ask to be run through with a spear so to end their pain, others seek forgiveness for their crimes, and then some curse and fume over the injustice done to them, yet I have never heard anyone, in all my years, ask for the forgiveness of those who were crucifying them."

"Many times over the days and weeks since Jesus' crucifixion, I have thought about His words. I can't tell

---

[53] Luke 23:34 (NIV).

you how many times I have asked God to forgive me for the role I played in His Son's death. I know I was only doing my duty as a Centurion, and I also know that I did it out of ignorance, but I did it nonetheless, and nothing can ever change that fact. I have grown in my knowledge and acceptance of forgiveness. I have experienced firsthand the love and grace of God over my actions, and because I know God has forgiven me, I have learned to leave it behind. This has helped me to find peace. You know it is sad, but some of the men in my cohort are still tortured by the events of that day. I try to help them see the truth of Jesus and how He forgave us, but they still struggle. Through this, I have found that it is hard for some people to accept His grace. I have accepted it, and because of His grace and forgiveness, I am no longer tormented as much by my actions. Of course, talking about it this evening has brought it all back to my memory, and it has been difficult to re-live, but it has been worth it. I feel that speaking about it for the record will help with the pain. I have also learned something more about forgiveness, and that is because I have been forgiven; I find it easier to forgive others when they do things to offend or anger me. When I think about holding a grudge, I remember Jesus' words, and I find myself uttering them as well—'Father, forgive them.'"[54]

At this, I nodded my head in agreement and thought to myself, in admiration of Octavian, for a man who has

---

[54] Luke 23:34 (NIV).

followed Jesus for only a short time, he has great understanding. I also thought it was nice to have Octavian, my brother in the Lord, back and not Octavian the Centurion. I like him much better as a brother.

Octavian continued by telling me about the criminals who were being crucified next to Jesus. "One of the criminals," he said, "Who had been mocking and jeering Jesus along with the other one, stopped when Jesus uttered the words, 'Father forgive them.' He rebuked the other criminal who kept hurling insults at Jesus and said. 'Don't you fear God?'[55] 'We are getting what we deserve... but this Man has done nothing wrong.'[56] He then said to Jesus, 'Remember me when you come into your kingdom.'[57] Jesus looked right at him and quite simply said, 'I tell you the truth, today you will be with me in paradise.'"[58]

"Standing there, a few feet away from the cross, I was moved in my heart by that criminal's words and the promise Jesus gave him. How could a beaten and dying man, suffering as Jesus was, still offer hope to another man, a criminal? When Jesus said those words about paradise and being with Him, I whispered to myself, *Me too*. I swear, Jesus, in all His fatigue and agony, looked right at me. Again, we caught eyes, and I real-

---

[55] Luke 23:40 (NIV).
[56] Luke 23:41 (AMP).
[57] Luke 23:42 (NIV).
[58] Luke 23:43 (NET).

ized He must have heard what I said, though they were spoken only in my head. It was eerie and amazing all at the same time. Everything for me changed at that very moment. My journey as a follower of Jesus, my Christ, began with those simple words. If it was that simple for a criminal and a Centurion, it must be for everyone else. All we had to do was ask Jesus if we could be with Him in paradise, and He said 'Yes.'"

I interjected at this time about my moment when I believed in Jesus. I reminded Octavian of how Jesus had healed me and then sent me on my journey back to the Decapolis to share the good news of what He had done for me. But before He sent me off, Jesus pulled me aside and asked if I believed that He was the Son of God, the Messiah. I said, "Yes, I believe," and so I know exactly how it felt to become a follower of Christ. Octavian then said, "That makes us brothers, right?" I smiled in agreement and then took a risk and said, "I'm not too sure that criminal considers you a brother." I braced myself, not sure if I should joke with a Centurion, but thank God he started laughing and said, "I would think not." *Whew*, I thought, we are making progress. Speaking of progress, I asked the Centurion what happened next.

"After Jesus looked at me and we had a connection, He turned His head and saw His mother standing near the cross, along with a few other women and a young man, whom I later found out was His disciple, John. Jesus looked at her and said, 'Woman, here is your son,' and to John, He said, 'Here is your mother.'[59] I was touched by this. Both Mary's and John's eyes were swollen with tears. I had to look away because my eyes were moistening up too. I did not want to appear weak or sympathetic to an insurrectionist in front of my soldiers. It was very difficult to maintain an indifferent disposition now, for I was feeling things I had never felt before, like empathy and compassion. Those indeed were the hours that changed my life."

"What was amazing about Jesus while He was on the cross was His presence of mind. For a dying man to think of others and not himself was so remarkable. Everything that happened that day, big and small, from His arrest to the Governor's palace to Skull Hill; when added up, all proved that Jesus was the Son of God."

I silently nodded and then asked Octavian if he had ever had the opportunity to meet Mary, the mother of Jesus. Octavian said, "Oh yes, John, as Jesus told him, cares for Mary and she is a regular at the gathering of the disciples." Octavian went on to say, "She is an amazing woman, always caring for and encouraging others. She always makes sure to greet me when she sees me. It is a privilege to know her, along with all the followers of Jesus. They are such wonderful people."

---

[59] John 19:26-27 (NIV).

CHAPTER 7

Darkness

Rubbing my hand a little but certainly not wanting to appear weak in front of Octavian, I stalled a bit and asked if he wanted more water. He said, "By the looks of things, you may need a little more water and a few moments to rest your hand." He reached out and took the pitcher of water and refilled my cup, then poured more for himself. I was taken aback, and he saw my reaction. He laughed and said, "I've told you, those were the hours that changed me; otherwise, you would have poured your own water. No offense, Justus, but prior to my encounter with Jesus, I would never have given a Jew a cup of water." I let out a chuckle, thanked him, and said, "No offense taken. In all honesty, before my encounter with Jesus, it probably would not have been water." We both laughed, and it felt good to be getting along so well with my new Centurion friend. I then asked Octavian, "So what happened next?"

He became quiet and seemed reflective. Looking upward and to the right, I could see he was searching for the right word. He shrugged a little, looked back at me, and uttered, "Darkness!"[60] I wondered what he meant because it was still in the middle of the day, so I said, "Darkness, in the middle of the day?" He then said, "Yes, and I mean darkness, the likes of which I had never before experienced. It was darker than a cave. A darkness you could feel—thick and cold, and it made my skin crawl. As you said, it happened right in the middle of the day. Just as we were crucifying God's Son, it felt like God turned off the sun."

"With the darkness came an eerie stillness. Everyone and everything became really quiet. It was unnerving. The wind became still because not even a breeze could be felt. Typically, there are sounds in the distance that one really pays no mind to like an occasional baby crying, a dog barking, or the normal sounds of people in the market places, but not now. When the sun stopped shining, everything in Jerusalem went deafeningly quiet. The mocking and berating by the religious leaders and the onlookers were all silent. The criminals on either side of Jesus made no sound. Everything felt very tense. Even the subdued sobs from Jesus' followers dissipated. Myself, along with my soldiers, were very quiet. I could tell they were frightened over what was happening. I think everyone was scared. I know I was,

---

[60] Mark 15:33.

and I do not frighten easily. Nothing like this had ever happened, nor do I believe will ever happen again."

"Then, all of a sudden, the silence of the darkness was broken as Jesus let out a loud and anguished cry, and His words pierced the darkness. Everyone in the area surrounding Skull Hill had to have heard Him because we were all startled! Jesus roared out these words that were the most disturbing I have ever heard. He screamed to the heavens, 'My God, my God, why have you forsaken me?'[61] At the sound of His voice, the hair on the back of my neck stood straight up. I didn't understand what was going on. Also frightening was the dead silence after His cry. That silence seemed even more deafening. He cried out to heaven, but there was no response, only the fading echo of His words. Jesus was now breathing very heavily, and He was having more and more difficulty catching His breath."

"The horror and fact of crucifixion are that the person slowly suffocates. When someone is nailed to a cross, the upper torso sags and the lungs are crushed by the body's weight. The only way to get a full breath is to push off the feet nailed to the pedestal and try to get your chest above the shoulders. This not only causes terrible pain in the feet but is also very tiring. Eventually, the person asphyxiates because they have no more strength left. At this time, Jesus was laboring quite in-

---

[61] Matthew 27:46 (NIV).

tensely, and I was wondering how much more He could, or should I say, would take. It was heart-wrenching to see Jesus in this state. I was already changing in my attitude and view of Jesus, and so I was feeling sorry for Him now. He was so alone. All the confidence, power, and true authority I had seen in Him earlier seemed to have disappeared. For the first time, He looked lost and confused."

I was a little lost and confused myself that Jesus was forsaken by God. I asked Octavian why he thought God would forsake Him? He said, "In talking with the disciples, they told me about the holiness of God and that when Christ was on the cross, all the sins of mankind were laid upon Him. It was at this time that our Father in heaven, being Holy, had to turn away from Jesus. Being an eyewitness to this event has been a chilling reminder that I pray God never turns away from me. Peter has told me that because of Christ, I never need to fear this happening. Jesus was forsaken by God for me. Peter also told me when he denied Jesus three times, a rooster crowed and Jesus looked right at him, but that it was a look of compassion rather than anger. I love hearing Peter's story and his vulnerability to be willing to share this painful part of his past. It reminds me of how Jesus often looked at me during those hours that changed my life. It was the same look of compassion and not anger or judgment."

I interjected that I, too, had heard Peter tell this story. "It amazes me how Jesus had turned Peter's weakness at that moment into such confidence for him. And a story that brings comfort and encouragement to others." Octavian agreed.

He then said, "The silence from Heaven was finally broken when Jesus said, 'I am thirsty.'[62] One of the soldiers fumbled around in the dark and found a sponge. He soaked it in some wine vinegar, set it on a hyssop branch, and lifted it up to Jesus' lips.[63] Jesus took a little of the wine vinegar, and it was then that I realized something. This was the only time in my whole encounter with Jesus that He asked for something for Himself. When accused or questioned, He was either silent or direct, or He was speaking up and defending others. I can't say it enough; He was, or should I say is, remarkable! He was as selfless a person as I have ever met. As I reflect on this now, Jesus only tasted enough of the wine vinegar to wet His lips. He didn't drink enough to satisfy His thirst, only enough to allow Him to speak His final words before He gave up His spirit."

"The darkness was giving way to the breaking dawn now. It seems strange to say 'dawn' when it was in the afternoon, but I don't know how else to describe it. I am not exactly sure how long it had been dark, only that the

[62] John 19:28 (NIV).
[63] John 19:29.

sun seemed to continue to travel across the sky, for it was near the position of the ninth hour. With the sun lighting up the day again, a rooster could be heard in the distance. The sound of the rooster made me realize just how quiet everything had been. It was like God had shut up or shut down everything in the city—maybe in the whole world. Could it be that God needed a moment of silence as His Son, Jesus, was dying on the cross?"

I just sat there dumbfounded by Octavian's observation. I said to Octavian, "You may be right. What if God in heaven made the world quiet while He contemplated the severity of His Son's death?" Octavian's perspective on the crucifixion of Jesus was proving more helpful than I could ever have imagined. I asked him to continue.

"With the rooster crowing and the sun beginning to shine again, it was as if life was re-emerging from the dead. Perhaps God had decided to give the world a second chance."

"Jesus said two other things before He expired. The first thing He said, as the sun was rising again, was, 'It is finished.'[64] At the time, I didn't understand what that meant because I had never heard of a man who was dying pronounce the end. I have since come to learn, from the help of the disciples, a few things about the meaning of these words. First, Jesus' words revealed the planning

---

[64] John 19:30 (NIV).

in all the events I witnessed during those long hours. None of what happened was by accident. The disciples have often spoken about all of the prophecies in the Scriptures regarding Jesus' death, and I can assure you, I bear witness to their fulfillment. As I previously said, Jesus died of His own accord. We did not take His life; He gave up His life for us... For me!"

"The other thing I learned about the words, 'It is finished,' is the deeper meaning. Jesus used the word 'te-telestai,' which is an accounting term used when a debt is fully paid. When I asked the disciples about this, they said that the world, all of us, owed a debt to God for the sins we had committed. In previous times, people offered sacrifices for their sins, but that those sacrifices didn't erase their sins. Jesus came to do this for us. He was the final sacrifice for all the sins of mankind, erasing them completely. 'It is finished' meant there was no more payment or sacrifice needed. We are all free if we choose His payment for our sin. I know a lot of people, especially Romans, who do not think they are sinners. They believe they are good people and therefore do not need a savior. If only they had witnessed what I was allowed by God to see when Jesus died on the cross, they might think differently about themselves, their sins, and the righteousness of Jesus."

"Since those hours that changed me, I have had several conversations with the disciple John, who was at the foot of the cross. We definitely have a special bond because of our shared experience. Anyway, he told me that he noticed Jesus looking at me a few times when He was on the cross, and because of that, he knew I had an encounter with Christ that day. The first time John saw me at one of the gatherings, he made sure to come up and introduce himself to me. I consider him not only a teacher in my life but a friend. Jesus is so amazing! He, in His death, made a Roman Centurion and a Jewish fisherman friends. The work of Jesus goes on and on. John, in one of our talks, said that 'It is finished' also meant Jesus had completed all He was sent by His Father to do. It was done! From the way He lived His life, to how He treated people, how He ministered to those in the masses, and to those who were all alone, and then finally in His death. He did what God commissioned Him to do. He finished."

"With that, Jesus then looked to heaven, and with the blood and the sweat streaming down His face, He mustered one last push upward to catch another breath and loudly proclaimed, 'Father, into your hands I commit my spirit.'[65] Then He simply bowed His head and breathed His last. It was over, finally. I was very sad and yet also relieved. I was mentally, emotionally, and physically exhausted. In an unusual sort of way, I was completely emptied out and yet had a sense of fullness I

[65] Luke 23:46 (NIV).

had never before experienced. I felt full in my heart and free of my past. All I could do was look up at Jesus on the cross, praise God, and declare to the world, 'Surely He was the Son of God.'"[66]

---

[66] Matthew 27:54 (NIV).

CHAPTER 8

The Aftershocks

There it was, Octavian's declaration that Jesus was the Son of God. I smiled, and then he smiled. "It is a powerful thing to say, isn't it?" "It sure is—the most powerful." I joked again that he was going to have to make his apologies to the thief on the cross when he got to heaven. He laughed and said, "There are a number of people with whom I will have to make amends."

"So after Jesus breathed His last," Octavian proceeded, "I took a deep breath, relieved that this day was finally over, but it wasn't. Several other things began happening. The most frightening and disturbing was the earth shaking under our feet and rocks splitting open all around the hillsides.[67] Earthquakes, if you have never experienced one, are very scary. You feel like the ground is ripping open and going to swallow you whole. I have been in a couple before, but the timing of this one, right after Jesus died, was no coincidence. Immediately, I felt I had done wrong for nailing Jesus to the cross, a

---

[67] Matthew 27:54.

sin I have repented of many, many times. Over the last few months, I have often reflected on these hours that changed my life and the astonishing events that surrounded Jesus' death. Just as the Pharisees had their plan, God also had His plan."

"Although I did not witness the two following occurrences, they have been confirmed to me, and I have no doubt that they happened. The first is the curtain in the Jewish temple was torn from top to bottom.[68] This is very significant as I have come to learn from the disciples. I am so grateful to these men who follow Jesus. They know so much about Him from His teachings and give such clear explanations of their Jewish culture and beliefs and how Jesus brought everything together. You probably already know this, but the curtain represented the separation between God and man due to our sin. Behind the curtain was the Ark of the Covenant, which is called the Holy of Holies. I was told that only the High Priest could go in there once a year to offer sacrifices for the sins of Israel. The disciples said that the torn curtain meant two important things. First, because of what Jesus did on the cross, there was no more need for a sacrifice for sins, and second, there was no longer any separation between God and man. All of this is because Jesus died on the cross for everyone. Of course, I had heard that the Pharisees were trying to deny the fact

---

[68] Matthew 27:51.

that this transpired, just as they denied Jesus rose from the dead. Fittingly, people scoff at the Pharisees now because of what they did to Jesus. They have lost so much credibility in Jerusalem that few people, if any, pay attention to them anymore. They still have their puppet followers who believe anything they say, but that crowd is growing smaller and smaller. The followers of Jesus, however, are increasing daily."

"The second remarkable thing that happened is that many tombs of the followers of God broke open, and although the people were dead, they were raised to life and were seen walking around praising God and bearing witness of Jesus.[69] Had someone told me this happened the day before, I would have scoffed in their face, but after the events I had seen and heard pertaining to Jesus, it was not only possible but not really that surprising."

"I then received word from a messenger that the Pharisees were complaining to Pilate about the bodies being left on the cross over their special Sabbath. They insisted to Pilate that the bodies be taken down and buried so as not to defile their sacred, holy day.[70] What the Pharisees still did not understand about Jesus and what happened during and after the crucifixion is that He is the sacred, Holy One to celebrate. Again, the reli-

---

[69] Matthew 27:52-53.
[70] John 19:31.

gious leaders missed the meaning of it all. They missed Jesus, the Messiah they were looking for!"

"The courier who was sent by Pilate informed me that the Governor wanted us to break the legs of the prisoners, so they would die faster and be removed from their crosses and taken away.[71] I then ordered the soldiers to break their legs, but when they came to Jesus, instead of breaking His legs, for we knew He had already expired, one of them took his sword and pierced His side. When he did, a mixture of blood and water flowed from Jesus, and I confirmed His death.[72] One of the disciples said that piercing Jesus' side fulfilled a prophecy from Zechariah."[73]

"What were you feeling during all of this?" I asked Octavian. He said, "Sorrow and joy, I guess. As I looked upon the body of Jesus, whom I had scarcely known before, I was struck by the horror and the beauty of it all. Throughout those several hours that I was on duty, fulfilling my obligations to Rome, I saw firsthand and even participated in the horror of what men can do to another man. I also was struck by the beauty of what Jesus did for humanity. Seeing all of this, I couldn't help but declare Jesus as the Son of God. I believed it to be true at the time and know it for certain today. I know Je-

---

[71] John 19:31.
[72] John 19:33-34.
[73] Zechariah 12:10.

sus died on that cross for me, for you, and for the whole world."

Octavian then balled up his fists and seemed to get quite agitated. I sat up a little straighter in my chair, worried that the Centurion might be back. I was relieved that he was only agitated about the Pharisees. He said, "I get so infuriated with the religious leaders because they tell people that Jesus either did not die or that if He did die, He did not rise from the dead. They are all liars! I witnessed His death, and I also know He rose from the dead. Whoever people choose to believe, the Pharisees or the disciples and actual witnesses, like myself, it is theirs to live with it. I just know what I know and have freely testified to the truth of these events."

I said to Octavian, "For the record, I believe this to be true as well." I then asked him, "So what happened after the blood and water flowed from His side?" He said something very interesting...

"Well, as we started to take the two criminals and Jesus down from their crosses, two men, one clearly wealthy and the other a religious leader, approached me and told me they had received permission from Pilate to take Jesus' body.[74] I was so relieved someone had come for Him. Later I learned that the two were named Joseph and Nicodemus. John and his adopted mother Mary, along with the other women, had left, and so I thought

---

[74] John 19:38-39.

we would have to dispose of Jesus' body—something I did not want to do."

"Typically, the removal of bodies was a mundane and unpleasant task performed by one of the subordinates, but Jesus did not deserve this kind of treatment. He needed to be treated with care and respect, so I was more than happy to release the body to the two men who had come for Him. When the soldiers finished removing Jesus from the cross, they carefully laid His lifeless form on the ground. I am fairly certain my men knew how I felt about Jesus, based on my declaration, so they handled Him with great respect. I noticed this and acknowledged their attention with an approving nod. Seeing Jesus' lifeless body just lying on the ground, I shook my head in disbelief. How could He be dead? A sadness I had never before felt hit me hard. With my knees shaking, I wobbled a bit and lost my balance. One of my soldiers who had taken Jesus' body down must have seen my trouble, and so he motioned for the two men who had come for Jesus to proceed. Joseph and Nicodemus stepped forward, stooped down, and began with great care to dutifully wrap His body with strips of linen and spices.[75] After all I had witnessed Jesus endure, I was having a hard time watching His body being covered. Within moments, I knew I would never see Him again. When the strips of linen covered His face and eyes, I

---

[75] John 19:40.

turned away. Now it was done. Oh, how I was going to miss His eyes! It made me sad to think I would never see them again. At the same time, I couldn't take my eyes off of Nicodemus and Joseph. I was deeply moved by what I was watching. The two moved with such grace, which spoke of their deep love and respect for Jesus. A picture flashed through my mind as they were wrapping Jesus' body with such precision and care. It was a picture of the soldiers who fold our banners or flags that we use to communicate on the battlefield. As a sign of respect for your cohort and for the Legions of Rome, the banners must be folded with the same great precision and care I saw from Joseph and Nicodemus. It felt like the banner for all humanity, the battle cry of God, was now being folded and put away. Then the two men took Jesus away, and I bowed my head and prayed a prayer of thanksgiving that it was over."

I was deeply moved by all of Octavian's words. Instantly I thought of Moses, and how he called Jehovah, His banner,[76] and then of Solomon, who wrote about how God's banner is love.[77] I mentioned this to Octavian, and he looked pleasantly surprised. I told him that those were some pretty astute observations. He said, "Thank you," and then went on to say...

---

[76] Exodus 17:15.
[77] Song of Solomon 2:4.

"Thankfully, clearing the Skull was not part of my detachment's duties. I did order a few of my soldiers to dispose of the other two men's bodies who were crucified. With Jesus' body carefully carried away, our task was complete and we started making our way back to the Praetorium."

"Physically exhausted, emotionally drained, and sick to my stomach, I led the remaining soldiers on the mile or so march. Even though exhausted to the core, I felt a sense of deep gratitude and fullness in my heart, maybe for the first time in my whole life, for my life had been pretty empty up until the moment I confessed Jesus as the Son of God."

CHAPTER 9

The Aftermath

I had never been happier for another human being as I was for Octavian at that moment. Seeing his face and his eyes welling up with tears, I couldn't help but be moved. He didn't try to hide those tears, either. Then, breaking the tension, I laughed and said, "What are we, a couple of babies?" He laughed too. I then asked him how his men were handling all they had witnessed. He said, "Some of them are confused but all of them were greatly impacted." I said, "How could they not be?"

Octavian then said, "Our march back to the barracks was in complete silence. The only sound that could be heard was the thud of our boots hitting the ground and our swords clanging at our sides. I know they, like me, were exhausted. There was not only the physical fatigue of being up most of the night and day, but we were also emotionally drained. When we reached our barracks, we cleaned up, I excused the men to their quarters, and I retired to mine."

"Sleep did not come easily or quickly. As tired as I was, the events of the day rolled around my mind. I tossed and turned all night, and I could not get the vision of Jesus on the cross out of my head. It was an awful night of sleep, or more accurately, no sleep. The next day I was still on duty, but thankfully, there wasn't much to do, so I was able to take it easy."

Octavian then mused, "I'm sure you know how it feels when you've had too much to drink the night before, and the next morning you feel like your head is going to split wide open, yes?" I confirmed that I was all too familiar with that feeling. Octavian said, "That was how I felt that morning."

He went on to say, "As I was milling about the Praetorium, I heard from Felix that our fellow Centurion, Ignatius, and his cohort had been assigned to guard the tomb where Jesus was laid. That seemed odd to me. Why would he be assigned to guard the tomb of Jesus? I asked Felix why and he relayed to me that the Pharisees were worried Jesus' disciples would steal the body and claim He rose from the dead, so they went to Pilate and asked for a guard to be posted.[78] Why was I not surprised? The Pharisees... always the Pharisees. They were so frightened and intimidated by Jesus. Of course, once you spent any length of time with our Lord, you couldn't help but feel a little intimidated. However, the Phari-

---

[78] Matthew 27:62-65.

sees were not afraid of Jesus in a good and respectful way; they were afraid of losing their power. In my many years of service to Rome and the years I spent stationed in Jerusalem, the one thing I have learned about people in power, religious or not, is that they definitely want to keep it. Jesus was a threat to people in power because He had real power that brought about real change, so I understand why the Pharisees were worried about Jesus rising from the dead and why they would want a guard posted. If Jesus rose from the dead, as He said He would, it would have been the ultimate display of His power. Death would no longer have the final say over mankind!"

"Very true!" I said to Octavian, "The Pharisees are sure in an uproar over Jesus rising from the dead, and for good reason. His resurrection has changed the world!" Octavian nodded in agreement and continued...

"Early the next day, the first day of the week, as I was in the yard of the Praetorium, Ignatius, who had just come in with his soldiers from the tomb where Jesus was laid, dismissed his men and briskly approached me. He pulled me aside as if to tell me a secret. Clearly, he was shaken up, very puzzled, and a little frightened. He was upset and talking very rapidly but in a lowered voice so as not to be overheard. I told him to take a deep breath, slow down, and tell me what was going on. After some shifting around and stuttering a bit, he finally just blurted it out, 'Jesus is gone!' Then he quickly covered his mouth and looked around as if he were in trouble. Well, technically, he was in big trouble."

"A Centurion, or any Roman soldier for that matter, did not "lose" someone they were guarding, especially a "dead" someone they were guarding, that is, if you wanted to live. You wouldn't even want to be found sleeping while on watch, must less lose someone. I asked him what happened, and he said, 'My soldiers and I were standing guard when all of a sudden an earthquake happened.' I nodded my head because I've seen this one before. Then he said, 'Suddenly, out of nowhere, an angel was standing right there in front of us!'[79] 'Wait, what?' I asked. 'Did you say an angel appeared?' He said, 'Yes! I have never been so frightened in my life. The appearance of the angel was terrifying and beautiful all at the same time.' I said, 'What did you say or do?' 'Nothing, we just stood there trembling.'"

I interrupted again and said to Octavian, "Mary Magdalene has also spoken of an angel she saw at the empty tomb. How awesome a sight that must be." Octavian said, "Not if you ask Ignatius, he was scared out of his wits." Although I have to say that as Ignatius was relaying all of this to me about the earthquake and the angel, a little smile formed on my lips. He, on the other hand, did not think it was all that amusing, but I ex-

---

[79] Matthew 28:2-4.

plained to him that I did not think it was funny, nor was I laughing at him. I assured him I was only pondering what he was saying. I told him that of all the things I had witnessed two days ago, it made absolute, perfect sense and that I did not think he was the least bit crazy. Ignatius then said the religious leaders paid them some money and told them to say they fell asleep and that someone came and stole the body.[80] They said that we would not get into trouble, and they would back our story if we were questioned. I looked at him, and then I said, 'Now I think you are crazy. First of all, if you were asleep, as you are supposed to report, how could you then know the body was stolen? You would have been asleep, and if you knew the body was being stolen, you would have stopped it, correct? So what the Pharisees are paying you to report makes no sense. What else makes no sense is to trust the Pharisees. Do you really think they will have your back?' Ignatius was in a real mess! The Pharisees had the soldiers over a barrel, and so they continued to spread the lie that Jesus' body was stolen and that He did not rise from the dead."

Octavian went on to say, "I felt bad for the jam Ignatius was in at that moment. He, along with many of the soldiers on duty the day of the crucifixion, were either grief-stricken or afraid over the whole situation. Sleep hadn't come easy for anyone in the barracks. Others

[80] Matthew 28:11-15.

were tormented in their minds by what they did to Jesus. Those who were not on duty the day of the crucifixion do not understand how any Roman soldier could be upset about the beating and crucifixion of an insurrectionist. I've tried to explain it to them, but they just don't get it. There are a few of the soldiers who are indifferent to everything relating to Jesus and what happened that day. They just go about their jobs as if the death of Jesus was routine. I can't judge them for this because I was indifferent to Jesus myself before those hours I spent with Him. Those hours that changed my life."

Leaning back in his chair and tilting his head upward, Octavian mused, "Jesus is such a polarizing figure. Some people, like myself, love and worship Him; some are completely unmoved by Him, and then there are those who hate Him. This has become even more true after the resurrection of Jesus from the dead. Some people believe, others doubt, and then some people, especially the religious ones, fight it, deny it, and mock it."

He continued, "The days following the resurrection, the whole city was up in arms. The word on the street was buzzing about the darkness, the earthquake, the empty tombs, and then the torn curtain. The real noise was still coming from the Pharisees. They were telling everyone that Jesus was a fraud and a hoax. They were also saying Jesus was filled with demons and therefore could not have risen from the dead. The disciples, at least for the first few days, were nowhere to be found. They must have been in hiding. I would have thought they would have immediately come out and defended Jesus, but there was not a word from them."

"As the week went on, the disciples could finally be heard in the city streets telling everyone that Jesus was alive and that they had seen Him. I had already chosen to believe Jesus was alive because of my experience with Jesus and because of what Ignatius told me. I was just glad the disciples were coming out of their hiding places and standing up for our Messiah. There were also many others who were bearing witness to Jesus' resurrection from the dead. They had such credibility because no one could fake the kind of joy in their eyes, and the fact that there were so many of them, made it difficult to refute. The Pharisees frantically tried to denounce all the witnesses as liars, but it is hard to tell someone who has seen something as phenomenal as Jesus, who has risen from the dead, that what they saw never happened. Countless people, over the coming weeks, saw Jesus alive and could not be silenced,[81] no matter how hard the Pharisees and others tried."

Octavian then leaned forward as a smile came across his face. He seemed excited to tell me something, and so I leaned in, excited to hear what he was about to say.

---

[81] 1 Corinthians 15:3-8.

It felt like a joy came over Octavian, and I couldn't help but feel his joy myself. So I asked him, "What happened next?"

"I almost want to start by telling you that... *You won't believe this,* but I think you will. Later that week, in fact, exactly one week after the arrest, trial, and crucifixion, I was off duty and at my home in the Roman section of Jerusalem. We have our own little enclave of Roman soldiers and palace workers. We have always preferred to be away from the Jews, and I know they prefer it that way too. Anyway, it was in the evening, the day before the Jewish Passover. I had just finished my evening meal and was getting ready to retire for bed when Jesus was, well, right in front of me! It was like He just walked through the walls of my house. I froze! Then instantly, out of what must have been sheer instinct, I fell at His feet in worship. Jesus let out a bit of a chuckle and helped me to my feet. Then He said in a playful tone, 'I remember when you did that in the Garden the day of my arrest. It's better to do so voluntarily, isn't it?' I sheepishly nodded, and He told me how glad He was to see me. He even called me 'Brother.'"

"I was awestruck and dumbfounded. He laughed again, and then I sort of laughed. I was so nervous in His presence, but He immediately put me at ease. I told Him I had just finished dinner, and He asked if there was anything left. I said 'Yes, and started to turn to get

Him something to eat, but He grabbed my arm and said He was fine and that He didn't want anything to eat but that He really came just to talk with me. He spoke to me for a few minutes, some of the things I will share with you, but some things are very personal, and I would like to keep them to myself."

I said to Octavian that I completely believed everything he was telling me to be true and that I was amazed he saw Jesus alive. I told him how I can't wait to see Jesus again and then asked Octavian to go on.

"First of all, I asked Jesus to forgive me for my part in His death. Jesus said, 'I know, I have heard you ask several times, and each time I have forgiven you—just as I forgave everyone while on the cross. I know you heard me say this because, like the good soldier you are, you were very observant of everything happening that day.' He also told me that I was one of the bright spots of the whole ordeal—seeing me so attentive and then moved by all that was transpiring made it all worth it for Him. I was a bit embarrassed by His words, but He was very sincere. He also said the other bright spot was the one on the cross who put His trust in Him. Again, I was amazed at Jesus. How He could even notice a soldier and a thief while dying on a cross is hard to imagine, but the more you spend time with Him, the less surprised you are by His love and goodness. Only those who want to go unnoticed by Jesus will, but anyone and everyone who wants to be seen and known by Him will be."

I told Octavian that I could not agree more and that I was not even looking for Jesus when He found me. Octavian said, "Nor was I. I guess we could say, 'He was searching for us.'" Again, I was struck by his wisdom and apologized for the interjection, which he waved off and continued...

"Hearing Jesus say He forgave me melted away all the shame I had been feeling the past few days. He also removed a lot of weight I had been carrying the past years over the things I had done in my service to Rome. All my sins and the grief caused by them were lifted from me that evening. I had never felt so free! Jesus told me, 'It is finished,' remember? He also confirmed to me that all the things I was thinking and feeling about Him during the arrest, trials, the beatings, and His time on the cross were, in fact, accurate. He then said, 'Octavian, the eyes are the window to the soul, and mine were reaching out to yours the whole time.' When Jesus told me this, I started weeping."

"Jesus then spent some time telling me who I really was and what my true calling was—to be a witness for Him. He also told me that as a Centurion, I was not only a guardian of Rome but that I am a guardian of His Word and His followers and I would do well to protect them."

I looked at Octavian and said, "I can't think of a better one." With that, Octavian said, "It is for this reason, I am so happy you asked me to speak with you about what I had seen and heard. I try to tell everyone who is seeking answers to life what Jesus has done for me. I know I still make mistakes. My temper, foul mood, and foul mouth still need His forgiveness daily, but I know, based on what He said to me, that He loves me, forgives me, and will never leave me. Often I am reminded by something Jesus called me that evening. He called me 'Brother.' Even though I do not have an earthly brother, as a soldier, I understand brotherhood. For Jesus to call me His brother means so much to me. When I am in front of my cohort and we are called to march into battle or a dangerous situation in my station at Jerusalem, I need to know my brothers, fellow Centurions, and cohort are behind me. A brother in arms, from my perspective, will always be there for you, and you must always be there for them. I now call Jesus my brother, too. As my commanding officer, I also call Him my King."

"There was one other thing Jesus told me that I must share with you. He told me to love people the same way He loved me.[82] Love for me has never been easy to give or receive, but with Jesus' help and the help of His disciples, we are working on it. I consider myself His work in progress, who is slowly making progress.

---

[82] John 13:34-35.

CHAPTER 10

The Journey Home

Octavian sat back and rubbed his eyes. As his hands pulled away from his face, he had a look of satisfaction, like his mission was complete. Taking this cue, I asked if he had said all he needed to say. He said, "Yes, I think that wraps it up. I can't believe I talked for so long, sorry about that." I shook my head and said I was willing to sit all night if need be to get his story written down and that I thought it was riveting. As Octavian was thanking me, I heard the voice of John apologizing for the interruption as he approached the table. I turned and said, "Perfect timing, John, we were just finishing up." John asked how everything was going, and Octavian said, "Very well." Octavian went on to tell John what a blessing it was to be able to finally have everything he witnessed documented. I nodded in agreement to John and told him I had learned so much from Octavian and was excited to share my findings with all the people at our gatherings back home in the Decapolis.

I asked John if he wanted to sit, but he declined and said, "I only wanted to see how the two of you were doing and ask how long you would be staying in Jerusalem." I said I would only be in the city for another day and that Lazarus, Martha, and Mary had invited me to dinner the next evening. Evidently, the three of them want to speak with me about the ministry back home to see if there is anything they can do to help. I told John I was also excited to talk with them about their experiences with Jesus, especially Lazarus. A bit of a wry smile formed on my lips as I said, "I'm dying to hear what it is like to be raised from the dead." Octavian, who was catching on to my humor, dropped his head in his hands and then turned to John and said, "You see what I have had to put up with this evening?" John rolled his eyes and said, "Trust me, I know Justus all too well." I then said, "Seriously, I do want to know their stories. One cannot gather enough information about the Lord." They both agreed.

John then turned his attention to me and said, "Justus, that was one of the reasons I stopped by the table. I was wondering if you had time to talk after you and Octavian are finished?" I told him that it was never too late in the evening to talk with him. Octavian, observant as always, took John's cue and chimed in that he was done and started to excuse himself from the table. John quickly said to the both of us, "Before you leave Octavian, I was hoping the two of you would permit me to have a copy made of your conversation. After all, it is your story Octavian and Justus; it is your writing." He continued, "Obviously, all of us disciples have our own experiences with Jesus, but that we are also trying to gather as much information as we can about Jesus from other eyewitness accounts. Everyone who had an encounter with Jesus needs their story told." I wholeheartedly agreed. Octavian, who had proved to be a very wise new follower, emphatically said, "It is not my story; it is all of our stories." I smiled and thought, *What a great man this Centurion was. Jesus knew what He was doing in choosing him.*

As the Centurion stood, John put his hand on Octavian's shoulder, and the two embraced. It still surprised me to see a Roman Centurion and a Jewish fisherman hug one another. I know the two were friends, but it was still an amazing sight to see. John could see the look on my face and said, "Jesus can make all sorts of people friends." At this, Octavian said, "Even brothers, right?"

I sat there thinking how remarkably close people can become when Jesus is the center of the friendship. Octavian was right; we were brothers, the family of God!

As I rose from the table, I thanked Octavian profusely for all the information he had given me and for allowing me to write down all his words. He, on the other hand, thanked me for giving him the opportunity to share his experience. I told him that his story would be put to good use back home in the Decapolis and that all the followers of Jesus were anxiously awaiting to hear the report.

I then went to shake Octavian's hand, but instead, he grabbed me and gave me a near bone-crushing bear hug. He turned to leave, and as he was walking away, he said, "Until we meet again, Brother."

My heart was so full as I stood there watching him go; it felt like I was already missing him. Octavian had said a few times how those hours with Jesus were the hours that changed his life. I took that to mean those hours had allowed him to discover the wonders of Jesus and commit his life to Christ. Even though I had committed my life to Jesus some time ago, I can say with certainty, my time with Octavian, and hearing his account of our Lord, has forever changed my life.

It was odd how energized and exhausted I was all at the same time. I had been writing so much, and my hand was aching, but what a wonderful encounter it was. I felt like I had learned so much about Jesus, and no less, from a Roman Centurion. I couldn't wait to get back to the Decapolis and share what I had learned with the people at our gatherings, but that would be a few days from now. I still had a couple of people I needed to see and to hear their stories of Jesus.

By this time in the evening, there were only a few people left milling about and talking with one another. I looked over at John, shaking my head, almost in disbelief. I invited him to pull up a chair and said, "Let's talk." He said, "You must be tired." I said I was and that it was a lot to take in, and even though my hand was aching, I was glad I had written it down and that I would not have to remember it all because I may forget some valuable information. Now that it is all recorded, it will be preserved. That is the beauty of writing important things down; you preserve them. John said, "This was why I asked Octavian and yourself if I could get a copy. We need to have a number of copies made so that they can be shared with other followers." I told John that I'd be happy to copy all of Octavian's words, just not that night. He laughed and said, "No, I suppose not." We agreed to meet up the next afternoon and that he would ask a few of the disciples to join us in making copies.

John then asked if we were having any problems with the Pharisees or religious leaders in the Decapolis. I told him there was some opposition, but not too much because the Jewish communities in our area were not as devout as the Jews in other areas, like Jerusalem. I said, "In spite of the little we had faced, we were finding great success and making huge strides in the region."

John told me they were having some problems due to their preaching about Jesus. I asked him if it was true some troublemakers were trying to outlaw even speaking the name of Jesus. "Can they do that, John?" "Not if you ask Octavian." John shook his head and chuckled. "That Octavian can sure live up to the name Calidus. He gets pretty angry over those Pharisees."

"I remind Octavian of Jesus' words about forgiveness, and he knows it is true, that we must forgive, but that it is still an ongoing battle for him. I guess for myself as well. I try not to push him too hard about forgiving, though. He is growing, but not fully grown."

John went on, "There is a particular Pharisee, a little younger than myself. He is very aggressive toward the followers of Christ. He was a disciple of Gamaliel and was well educated and a skillful debater. He is arguing with us almost daily and trying to have those who proclaim Jesus as Lord arrested. He is also making threats of going to other towns to put a stop to the followers of Jesus. He then said he was only telling me this to be on the lookout.

I asked John how concerned he was and if he thought they were in danger. John shrugged and said, "Jesus warned us about all of this happening, so it is no real surprise. It is a little scary when you are going through it, though, but the Holy Spirit, our Comforter, is always with us, as Jesus promised!"[83]

---

[83] John 14:16.

I asked John if there was anything I could do to help, but he said, "No, not at this time." He did ask me, however, to stay vigilant and continue to pray. Jesus would often tell us, "Watch and pray."[84]

With that, the two of us embraced, and I turned to make my way back to the home of my friend on the outskirts of Jerusalem. I thought as I left, *I will sleep well tonight.*

Making my way through the courtyard, for some reason, I turned and called back to John, "Do you remember the name of that Pharisee who is causing the followers all the trouble?" John hollered back, "It's probably nothing, but his name is Saul of Tarsus."

Huh! I thought, never heard of him...

---

[84] Luke 21:36.

Epilogue

If you have never declared Jesus, the Son of God, like the Centurion Octavian, you are just a prayer away from the greatest and best relationship you could ever know.

As a minister of the Gospel for thirty-three years, I have performed many, many weddings. At every wedding I have ever performed, I always ask this very important question. Turning to the groom, I say, "Do you take this woman to be your lawfully wedded wife?" and then I wait for his response. When he says, "I do," I turn to the bride and ask the same question of her, waiting for her response. When she says, "I do," I tell them that in the eyes of God, their profession begins their marriage. I want you to know that before the world was created, Jesus said, "I do" to you, and He is waiting for your response.

The Apostle Paul tells us, "If you declare with your mouth, 'Jesus is Lord,' and believe in your heart that God raised Him from the dead, you will be saved. For it is with your heart that you believe and are justified, and it is with your mouth that you profess your faith and are saved. As the Scripture says, 'Anyone who believes in Him will never be put to shame."[85] It is just that simple. Jesus did all the work on the cross for us so that it would be by grace, His grace.

Now that you have confessed Jesus as your Lord and Savior, "It is finished," as far as you being completely forgiven and a member of God's family, but your journey in Christ is just beginning. To further your relationship with Jesus, it is essential to find a Bible-believing teaching and preaching church to help you form good relationships within God's family, or as Octavian would call them, "Brothers". The second essential is to get yourself a copy of a Bible—either in a bookstore or online. I prefer using the New International Version, the NIV for short, but there are so many good translations of God's written Word. It could be helpful to ask your new local church what translation they prefer. The important thing is to get a Bible and start reading it daily. At our church in Gilroy, CA., we do what we call the "Cover-to-Cover Campaign." I provide our church with bookmarks that have daily readings from the Old Testament and New Testament. You can find them on our website... www.thefoothillschurch.org.

I also encourage our church to read a few chapters from the book of Psalms every day and the Proverb of

---

[85] Romans 10:9-11 (NIV).

the day. There are 31 chapters in the Book of Proverbs, one for each day of the month. Until you find a good local church, you can follow along with my weekly sermons on our web page or YouTube.

God bless you on your journey, and may we see many more people like Octavian, Justus, and the many disciples of Jesus, before His return.

References

The Holy Bible: Amplified Bible [AMP]. 2015. La Habra, California: The Lockman Foundation. https://www.biblegateway.com/versions/Amplified-Bible-AMP/#booklist.

The Holy Bible: English Standard Version [ESV]. 2007. Wheaton, Ill: Crossway Bibles. Public domain. https://www.biblegateway.com/versions/English-Standard-Version-ESV-Bible/#booklist.

The Holy Bible: New English Translation [NET]. 2006. Biblical Studies Press. https://www.biblegateway.com/versions/New-English-Translation-NET-Bible/#vinfo.

The Holy Bible: New International Version [NIV]. 2011. Grand Rapids: Zonderman Publishing House. https://www.biblegateway.com/versions/New-International-Version-NIV-Bible/#booklist.

The Holy Bible: New Living Translation [NLT].
2013. Carol Stream: Tyndale House Foundation. Tyndale House Publishers, Inc.
https://www.biblegateway.com/versions/
New-Living-Translation-NLT-Bible/#booklist.

The Holy Bible: The New King James Version [NKJV].
1999. Nashville, TN: Thomas Nelson, Inc.
https://www.biblegateway.com/versions/
New-King-James-Version-NKJV-Bible/#booklist.

About the Author

Mark S. Wilson, and his wife of thirty-nine years, Joani, have pastored "The Foothills Church" in Gilroy, CA., for thirty-one years. Mark and Joani have two sons, Brooks and Chad, a daughter-in-law, Jillian, and two grandkids, Noah James and Ava Grace.

Mark graduated in 1978 from Dallas High School in Dallas, Oregon. He also attended George Fox University in Newberg, Oregon, and Mesa State University in Grand Junction, Colorado. It was in Grand Junction where he committed his life to Christ at the New Horizon's Foursquare Church. That evening he also received his call into full-time ministry. To prepare himself for the ministry, he went to L.I.F.E. Bible College in Los Angles, CA., and received his B.A. in Theology in 1985. Upon graduation, Mark went on staff as a youth pastor at Florence Avenue Foursquare Church under the direction of Dr. Paul Risser. Aside from loving his family and The Foothills, Mark loves to golf and fish and is an avid San Francisco Giants and Golden State Warriors fan.

CPSIA information can be obtained
at www.ICGtesting.com
Printed in the USA
FSHW021516071221